D0891486

READERS AND MYTHIC SIGNS

·

the Oedipus myth

IN TWENTIETH-CENTURY FICTION

Debra A. Moddelmog

SOUTHERN ILLINOIS
UNIVERSITY PRESS
Carbondale and Edwardsville

Edited by Patricia St. John-Doolin

Designed by David Ford

Production supervised by Natalia Nadraga

96 95 94 93   4 3 2 1

Library of Congress Cataloging-in-Publication Data
Moddelmog, Debra.
  Readers and mythic signs : the Oedipus myth in twentieth-century
fiction / Debra A. Moddelmog.
     p.   cm.
  Includes bibliographical references and index.
    1. Fiction—20th century—History and criticism. 2. Oedipus
(Greek mythology) in literature. 3. Reader-response criticism.
4. Mythology—Psychological aspects. 5. Psychoanalysis and
literature. I. Title.
PN3503.M52   1993   92-34304
809.3'915—dc20   CIP
    ISBN 0-8093-1846-6

The paper used in this publication meets the minimum requirements of
American National Standard for Information Sciences—Permanence of
Paper for Printed Library Materials, ANSI Z39.48-1984. ♾

Portions of chapter 4, "Mythemes and Questions of Genre: The
Blindness of the Private Eye in Antidetective Fiction," have been
previously published in revised form as "The Oedipus Myth and Reader
Response in Pynchon's *The Crying of Lot 49*" in *Papers on Language
and Literature* 23.2 (1987). Copyright © 1987 by the Board of Trustees,
Southern Illinois University. Reprinted by permission.

For my parents

Contents

■

Contents

Acknowledgments

∎

I would like to thank everyone who read and commented on all or parts of this book at various stages of its progress: Phil Young, Robert Secor, Chris Catalano, Mac Davis, Katherine Burkman, Jeff Yule, Jeredith Merrin, Diane Furtney, Sari Champagne; and the members of the Ohio State English Department Novel Group: Marlene Longenecker, Mark Conroy, Audrey Jaffe, Dick Martin, Linda Raphael, Anne Neumann, Barbara Rigney, and Murray Beja. I also appreciate the feedback from students in two Ohio State comparative literature classes with whom I shared some of the arguments advanced in this book. In addition, I owe a great deal to Mary Wehrle, my research assistant, who went beyond the call of duty in collecting information and helping to compile the bibliography.

In the course of my work on this project I received two Scholarly Research Assignments that enabled me to devote my time to writing, and I thank the Ohio State English Department and the College of Humanities for those opportunities. Curtis Clark of Southern Illinois University Press treated me and my manuscript with professional care, and I am grateful for his efforts. I also received invaluable guidance from the readers for Southern Illinois University Press, especially Eric Gould, and thank them for their input and encouragement. I also thank Patty St. John-Doolin for her careful editing of my manuscript and Susan Wilson for all her work on my behalf.

My deepest gratitude goes to Kathryn Hume, who provided superior direction during the initial stages of this project and continuous good advice, and to Jim Phelan, whose copious and insightful suggestions on several drafts greatly improved my work. The support of both of these scholars and friends has kept me going.

Acknowledgments

I have received unconditional support and love from my family, and I thank them for their encouragement, confidence, and constant good humor.

Finally, Ruth Ann Hendrickson has remained steadfast in her belief in me and my work and has talked me through every chapter. I thank her for understanding and for always being there.

Introduction: Reading Myth from Joyce to Pynchon

■

From James Joyce to Thomas Pynchon, Virginia Woolf to Flannery O'Connor, Thomas Mann to Alain Robbe-Grillet, William Faulkner to Alberto Moravia, Toni Morrison to James Welch, twentieth-century writers have been fascinated with myth and its possibilities in fiction. Critics, however, have not always shared the fascination. Since the 1950s and 1960s when critics like Northrop Frye, Philip Wheelwright, and Richard Chase made it fashionable to talk about the relationship of myth to fiction, myth criticism has declined in prevalence and, for some scholars, in relevance. In part this decline can be attributed to the very phenomenon that made mythic approaches popular in the first place: the changing nature of literary criticism. As we revise our understanding of literature and our relationship to it, we develop new approaches to accommodate these theories, and as a result, "older" perspectives are often seen as not only unfashionable but wrong. To paraphrase John Vickery, the scholar examining myth today looks like a country mouse next to those town architects developing and practicing feminism, new historicism, structuralism, and deconstruction.[1]

Yet some good reasons exist for not casting out myth criticism from our community of critical approaches. Most obvious among them is that myth has attracted many writers of this century, including those writing very recently. To ignore myth is to miss their interest and to dismiss an essential part of their work. A more sensible response to the future of myth criticism is the approach that Vickery advocates: to consider whether our revised knowledge of

literature and consciousness may enable us to reconstrue the relationship between myth and literature and thus to improve our com-
prehension of what happens when we create and read literature and
when we think about and use myth.[2] In regard to fiction, such
revisionist efforts have been undertaken since 1970, with critics such
as Vickery, William Righter, Jacqueline de Weever, and John White
focusing on the ways that fiction writers have used myth in the
twentieth century.

But despite this positive direction in myth criticism, most critics
continue to treat myth in fiction from the vantage point of author
first, reader last (or not at all). This approach begs many crucial
questions, from the most evident—Can myth play any role unless a
reader recognizes its presence?—to the most controversial—What
constitutes validity in interpretation when myth is involved? In
our current critical climate where poststructuralist theories have
challenged the autonomy of the text and where some critics are
arguing that the text is always only a projection of the reader, these
practical questions have immense theoretical repercussions. Most
importantly, they force us to rethink how we address the matter of
a myth's functions in fiction. As Vickery acknowledges, specific
"uses" of a myth in certain literary works are "perhaps preeminently,
a function of the critical activity, of consciousness as constitutive, of
the reader as 'formularizing' agent."[3]

So far as I know, only White has attempted to describe systemati-
cally the dynamics of reading "mythological fiction."[4] Yet while his
studies have turned attention to the reader, they have not adequately
dealt with all areas of the reader's participation. For one thing, they
center primarily upon what happens *as* we read such fiction and do
not help us to understand what also happens *after* we read these
narratives—the point at which interpretation becomes more deliberate. White himself concedes that we must go outside myth criticism—to the reader-response investigations of Wolfgang Iser[5] and
the personal hermeneutics of Roland Barthes in *S/Z*—to find models
that might help to explain the reasoning process a reader follows in
interpreting mythological fiction. However, because these models
describe reading in general or the experience of an individual reading

a single text, they cannot tell us much about the general case presented by the narrative using myth.

My central purpose in this study is to develop that case, to set forth a theory about how readers recognize and make sense out of a myth's appearances in modern fiction. Ideally my aim is explanatory: to describe the conditions and conventions that enable and empower interpretation of fiction that contains myth. I am aware, however, that theories, whether about reading or about natural phenomena, are never purely empirically derived, that they will necessarily reflect the presuppositions of their author. Stanley Fish has gone so far as to claim that theories about reading will always be fulfilled, for "they will always produce exactly the results they predict, results that will be immediately compelling to those for whom the theory's assumptions and enabling principles are self-evident."[6] But although Fish is right to warn us that theories influence perceptions, he overstates the case by ignoring that perceptions also influence theories. By exploring the reading habits of a number of readers,[7] we can locate shared methods of interpretation, if not always shared interpretations. Moreover, if one of the ways we become better readers is to understand how we read, others are to learn new reading strategies and to improve old ones. Hence, for those readers who believe that myth criticism always reduces the text or that, like bell-bottoms, it went out of style in the 1970s, I hope to prove otherwise, to show that such an approach can actually be highly stimulating and necessary, engaging us in all sorts of questions, quests, and conclusions.

The theoretical portion of this book (chapters 1 and 2) follows a structuralist program to the extent that it attempts to identify the elements involved in the production of meaning, to formulate a poetics, for fiction using myth. However, as Robert Scholes points out, structuralism can "make us keenly aware of the communicative aspects of the entire poetic process. But it will not read the poem for us. That we shall always have to do for ourselves."[8] Thus, in chapters 3, 4, and 5, I attempt to elucidate the poetics I have proposed by examining twentieth-century fiction in which the Oedipus myth appears. Inevitably the analyses of these chapters derive from my own contemplations of the fiction and myth; invariably some readers will suggest other ways to interpret the appearances of the Oedipus myth, its "mythemes," in these works. While such differences of opinion are common among readers, we can expect them to be especially prevalent wherever myth is involved, for as I explain in chapters 1 and 2, it is the nature of myth to elicit multiple meanings. Still, even those readers who dispute my ends in chapters 3–5 (my interpretations of various mythemes) should gain a better sense of the means by which these ends are reached (the dynamics of the interpretive process in general).

In chapters 3–5, I also explore various interpretive issues that arise in relation to the genres being studied. Chapter 3 (on science fiction works written by H. G. Wells, Jules Verne, Philip José Farmer, and Philip Dick and Roger Zelazny) reveals not only how a single mytheme can evoke a complex reading experience but also how each reading of a work containing a particular myth influences the next reading of a similar work. Chapter 4 (on antidetective fiction and works written by Alain Robbe-Grillet, Michel Butor, and Thomas Pynchon) addresses genre questions that the mytheme as structural unit calls forth. Chapter 5 (on psychological fiction written by Flannery O'Connor, Max Frisch, and Alberto Moravia) looks at the appropriation of the Oedipus myth by psychoanalysis and the consequences of that appropriation for those of us reading and writing after Sigmund Freud.

Finally, this study attempts to add to our understanding of the Oedipus myth and its appeal to the twentieth century. According to Northrop Frye, "the more we study the literary developments of a myth the more we learn about the myth"[9]; and in the first part of this book, I introduce specific principles for accepting and carrying out this assumption. The decision to look at fictional works using the Oedipus myth is not, however, simply an arbitrary or a convenient one. George Steiner observes that after 1905, under the pressure of Freudian reference, *Oedipus the King* became the Greek source that most interested artists and intellectuals.[10] Recently, Peter Rudnytsky has "corrected" Steiner's assessment, maintaining that Freud's unfolding of the Oedipus complex, "while marking a watershed in the history of ideas, must itself be seen as the climax of a long-standing cultural preoccupation with [*Oedipus the King*]. . . . [T]he widespread nineteenth-century interest in both *Oedipus the King* and *Antigone* is itself part of the larger phenomenon indelibly named by E. M. Butler 'the tyranny of Greece over Germany.'"[11] Oedipus' recurring appearance in modern fiction seems to support Steiner's and Rudnytsky's judgments that *Oedipus the King* has captivated writers of this century. But contrary to the impressions of many people, this fiction is not always grounded in Freudian psychology; indeed, for reasons I will explain later, I have generally excluded the family romance, the kind of story that most people probably think of as Oedipal.[12]

Even without these stories, Oedipus is a prolific presence in twentieth-century fiction, and so one can surmise that our age has found him fascinating for reasons other than, or in addition to, those proposed by Freud. Although many scholars have sought the source of Oedipus' appeal beyond Freud,[13] few have done so by investigating his appearances in twentieth-century fiction.[14] As the preceding chapter synopsis indicates, the Oedipus myth has surfaced most frequently in three kinds of twentieth-century fiction: dystopian science fiction, anti-(or metaphysical) detective fiction, and psychological fiction. If nothing else, we should want to know why the myth has been distributed in this way and if the distribution itself reveals something about the myth. Further, as Patrick Mullahy observes, "Myth has a history and cannot rightly be understood otherwise. It is fluid, never completed, adapted by successive generations to their religious, cultural and ethical standards, that is, in psychoanalytical language, geared to the current stage of psychic repression of the population."[15] One must obviously move carefully when drawing conclusions from a study of limited scope; but keeping in mind the need for caution, in the final chapter I explore further the reasons for our attraction to Oedipus.

Readers and Mythic Signs

C H A P T E R   1

Myths and Their Signs

■

Defining *myth* is as difficult as defining modernism and postmodernism or, at times, the difference between the Democrat and the Republican parties. So Herculean has this task become that some critics have chosen to dispense with it altogether. For example, William Righter declares that he will "abandon the futile effort to capture the elusive essence of [myth]" and will instead examine the variety of uses to which modern writers have put it.[1] John Vickery takes a similar empirical approach when he states that "pointing to the story of Orpheus is . . . indubitable as to what one means by a myth."[2] But such a rationale is more a rationalization and says, in effect, "I don't know what a myth is, but I know one when I see one." That expedient may move us along, but it will not move us very far toward understanding how an author "uses" myth or a reader "actualizes" it, since in both cases we need to know what exactly is being used and what is being actualized.

G. S. Kirk suggests that all that "is prudent to accept as a basic and general definition [of myth] is 'traditional tale,'" and in developing this idea, he writes:

> First, [traditional tale] emphasizes that a myth is a story, a narrative with a dramatic structure and a climax. . . . Myth-making is a form of story-telling. Second, "traditional" is significant because it implies, not only that myths are stories that are told especially in traditional types of societies . . . , but also that they have *succeeded* in becoming traditional. Not every tale . . . is found attractive or important enough to be passed from generation to generation. A tale must have some special characteristic for this

1

to happen, some enduring quality that separates it from the general run of transient stories.[3]

This analysis contains several key points about myth that can help to clarify the position of both the reader and the writer of twentieth-century fiction. To begin, narrative is intrinsic to myth. This means that for author and reader, a myth is not just a stock of characters and events but rather such a stock rendered into a specific relationship to each other through a particular act of telling. And yet *myth* is not synonymous with *story*. It is a particular kind of story that has "some special characteristic," "some enduring quality" that causes one generation to pass it on to the next; that inspires writers of each age to reshape it "in accordance with the needs and character of its climate";[4] and that puzzles readers from all sorts of disciplines into trying to understand it.

Identifying what makes myth "mythic" has engaged scholars for years, and to a large extent the answer to this question has been, and must continue to be, formulated deductively rather than inductively—as Righter and Vickery seem to realize in their decisions not to define myth. That is, no student of myth can come to the subject of "mythicity" completely free of preconceptions about what myth is or ignorant of various bodies of myths (mythologies) associated with different cultures. Thus, explanations of mythicity grow out of each scholar's knowledge of specific myths; and since, as Kirk reminds us, "the thousands of particular stories to which the name 'myth' is commonly applied cover an enormous spectrum of subject, style and feeling,"[5] one can easily see why we have almost as many definitions of *mythicity* as of *myth*.[6]

But although we cannot fully escape this circular reasoning of the relationship between myth and mythicity, we should still be able to develop an understanding of myth that will distinguish myth from narrative, even as we recognize that the line between those two entities is unstable and that we are dealing with a continuum rather than with absolute categories. Eric Gould argues that "literature and myth must exist on a continuum by virtue of their function as language: myth tends to a literary sense of narrative form, and fictions aspire to the status of myth. "[7] Gould thus locates the motive for myth in the conditions of language itself "and especially in the fact that language is a system of substitutions allowing the indefinite play of signification" (186–87). By connecting mythicity to semiotics and interpretation theory, Gould suggests that the "special characteristic" that separates narrative and myth is the human desire to express the inexpressible or to know the unknowable. As he states,

> Myths apparently derive their universal significance from the way in which they try to reconstitute an original event or explain some fact about human nature and its worldly or cosmic context. But in doing so, they necessarily refer to some essential meaning which is absent until it appears as a function of interpretation. . . . [T]here can be no myth without an *ontological gap between event and meaning.* (6)

Myths are consequently sites of "infinite metaphorical play trying to solve the social, sexual, and psychological compromises which create our civilized nature" (183).

But if there can be no myth without an ontological gap between event and meaning, there can also be no gap without a reader who perceives it as such. In other words, the "essential meaning" to which Gould refers is absent only because a reader intuits it to be so. A story approaches the mythic when it touches some need or desire or concern that a reader is unaware of and comes to recognize only through the experience of reading the story. When the story touches such a chord in a number of readers and then in several generations of readers, it has moved even further into the realm of the mythic, for it then becomes a metalanguage for expressing the inexpressible for an entire society. As Marcel Detienne puts it, "Why is it that what is called 'myth' resides in or is possessed by a need to discuss, a wish to know, to search out the meaning, the reason for its own manner of speaking?"[8]

Gould's conception of mythicity enables him to suggest that a myth can as easily originate in the modern world as in ancient or primal times; but we must also keep in mind that, whatever its origin, a myth is made, not born. It is, as Roland Barthes puts it, "a type of speech chosen by history."[9] Because a myth invites interpretation, including the interpretation of retelling and translation, it entices but never allows us to close the ontological gap that makes it mythic. In brief, myth is discourse that generates discourse and thereby brings with it an elaborate literary and interpretive history.[10]

A myth's history of interpretation and retelling is crucial to our purposes because it supplies material for authors to shape and/or readers to infer. Scholarly analyses of a myth become well known, some becoming more famous than the myth. As a result, mythic figures and tales carry their own catalog of psychoanalytic, anthropological, philosophic, theologic, aesthetic, and historical associations and speculations. A fiction writer may exploit one, several, or none of these meanings, but they are always latent in the myth so that whether or not the author does something with them, the reader may. Moreover, each new telling as well as each translation of a myth is an interpretation and can affect the modern author's handling or the reader's actualization of the myth. As George Steiner states, "The most learned classical scholar and the layman with his fallible translation are *both* the products of a massive history of inheritance. They come long after. Whether or not they are explicitly aware of the fact, the aggregate of preceding editorship, exegesis, staging, and criticism presses upon their own understanding."[11]

To summarize: a myth is a narrative, recurring in various forms throughout a significant period of cultural history, which has acquired, and continues to invite, a number of diverse meanings as readers seek to identify the psychic, social, or sexual unknown that the myth expresses. These meanings are typically proposed by readers working within such disciplines as anthropology, sociology, history, philosophy, psychology, and comparative religion as well as comparative mythology and literary criticism. Yet these analyses do not close up the myth, explaining it to everyone's satisfaction; in fact, they are likely to provoke further interpretations by compelling other readers to enter the dialogue surrounding the myth. Like a snowball rolling down a hill, a myth sustains its mythic nature, in part, by the build-up of commentary that inspires further transformation and interpretation of the myth.[12] A myth is thus polymorphous and intertextual, as well as (apparently) infinitely interpretable.

Despite a myth's multiplicity of form and meaning, an author can still choose and a culture can still privilege a particular version or interpretation. The reader who wishes to understand the modern story as the author constructed it will try to identify the version that the story relies upon and the interpretation(s) being invoked. But because the variants of a myth share universals (e.g., Oedipus killing his father and sleeping with his mother; Persephone being abducted by Hades), the reader might also find that such identification will simply lead to other versions, other interpretations. "There are no myths," according to Reuben A. Brower, "only versions . . . only texts for interpretation."[13]

The Oedipus myth presents an interesting case for study not only because our contemporary world has raised Oedipus to a position held by few mythic heroes but also because this raising results from knowledge of a single source: Sophocles' Theban trilogy. Our educational system—especially high school and college humanities classes—and Freud—who based his theories about infant development upon Sophocles' *Oedipus the King*—have together promoted Oedipus so that even the not so well read are acquainted with him. As Alister Cameron points out, although we know of eight ancient plays called *Oedipus*, "surely there is only one *Oedipus*," that of Sophocles.[14] For the twentieth century, one version of the Oedipus myth has become The Oedipus Myth. Although we must remember that neither writers nor readers are committed to drawing from Sophocles' presentation, we can still simplify and say that for the twentieth century Sophocles created Oedipus.

Myth as a Language

Created is a strong word, however, and it seems less extravagant and more accurate to say that Sophocles has written the "language" of Oedipus. This revision does not instantly clarify matters, since I have already connected myth to language, and since others such as Roland Barthes and Claude Lévi-Strauss have proposed similar associations. Most obviously, I am not reiterating the common idea that a myth is a symbolic language containing some hidden "message"—be it historical, psychoanalytical, metaphysical, societal, cosmological, or whatever—for as we have just seen, each myth carries all meanings that scholars have hypothesized for it while simultaneously remaining open to interpretation. A myth's true meaning is the paradox that it is meaning-full and meaningless at the same time. Rather, I am proposing that every myth functions in fiction as its own self-contained sign system. To state this from the reader's viewpoint, I am suggesting that readers identify and make sense out of myth in fiction in the same way that they recognize and interpret linguistic signs.

Already we have seen at least two ways in which myth acts like a language. First, if a myth is attended by a collection of analysis, then any time that myth appears in a narrative, it has the potential to transmit one or more of these adjunct interpretations. Second, if myth remains perpetually open to interpretation, then its presence in a work of fiction can always suggest new meaning. This power of myth to transfer as well as call forth meaning is comparable to that possessed by any highly charged discourse—for example, a poem— but corresponds most closely to the properties of a word rich in connotation. Such a term bears several meanings, any of which a writer may exploit, but is also likely, as John Parry points out, "to give rise to ambiguity, since there can be no guarantee that in using it the same attributes will be in the minds of speaker and listener."[15]

But the assertion that formal analyses of a myth can be communicated to readers needs qualification. The fact is that most scholars do not interpret the entire myth but extract parts of it to support their own arguments. Indeed, the nineteenth and twentieth centuries might be seen as the age that destroyed myths only to give their fragments new meaning.[16] Richard Chase, for instance, writes of the "paramyth," "[a] philosophical concept, a moral allegory, a symbol seized upon, cut off from the living whole."[17] Perhaps the most famous example of this extirpation is the practice of psychoanalysis,

6

which arrests the development of figures such as Oedipus and Narcissus by turning them into stages of personality growth. Freud's Oedipus especially seems a distorted image of Sophocles' king and has provoked some critics to argue that Freud misunderstood Sophocles (although, ironically, a few of these critics misunderstand Freud). Similarly, Freud's Narcissus is a youth frozen in time, unable to escape that day when he looked into a pool.

As a consequence of this fragmentation, certain interpretations apply only to certain sections of the myth, and even interpretations that cover the whole myth can often be divided along these splintered lines. For instance, Freud's Oedipus has very little to do with a riddle or the Sphinx, but everything to do with mother-son love and father-son rivalry. In contrast, psychoanalyst Victoria Hamilton has recently heightened the importance of Oedipus' search for personal identity and lessened the significance of his marriage.[18] This vivisection of myth by scholars parallels the common practice of most fiction writers who use a myth not by dropping it intact into their story (or by retelling it as many dramatists and poets do) but by borrowing and integrating parts of it to illuminate their narrative.[19] Because both scholars and writers are dividing up myths, we cannot assume when a myth appears in a story that all the myth's critical interpretations come along. Partial interpretations remain with the section of the myth to which they pertain; still, the essential point is that these interpretations can be relayed—or inferred.

The fragmenting of myth by scholars and authors should not imply that myth has become like Humpty-Dumpty, never to be put together again. Actually, when writers incorporate any part of a myth into their narrative, readers typically repair the myth, and most authors rely upon this reconstruction. To be more specific, a segment of a myth introduced into a narrative asks readers to compare part of the modern story to an incident in the ancient one, thus opening up potentialities for the rest of the narrative, the most obvious being that the story will follow the sequential patterning of the myth.[20] The author can either satisfy or frustrate these possibilities, but whatever the result, the fact that they are raised at all indicates that

7

the memory stores the myth as a whole. Authors and scholars may sever the myth; however, the fragments are not amputated limbs, but advertisements promoting their origin.

This is simply to say that mythic characters and scenes inhabit our imaginations as parts of, rather than apart from, their mythic milieu. Such retention has been reinforced by our experience of reading novels such as James Joyce's *Ulysses*, Thomas Mann's *Joseph and His Brothers*, Agatha Christie's *The Labours of Hercules*, and John Updike's *The Centaur*. In other words, these mythological novels have helped to form the habit of recovering the entire myth when we meet with one of its parts. Such habit formation accompanies the genesis of any genre, which, as Jonathan Culler states, "the author can write against, certainly, whose conventions he may attempt to subvert, but which is none the less the context within which his [and here we can add the reader's] activity takes place."[21] Our training as readers thus supports our natural tendency to see myth as a whole composed of interrelated parts. Moreover, this habit of calling forth the entire myth when we meet with any of its parts has important consequences for the myth as well as for the narrative; for if it is true that the myth tells us something about the modern story, it is equally true that the narrative's appropriation of the myth causes us to reinterpret the myth. Had Joyce written only Molly Bloom's final monologue and presented Molly as a Penelope figure, we would still find ourselves remembering and reassessing the Odysseus myth from beginning to end (although, of course, the significance of that reevaluation would almost certainly be different from the one we undertake with the novel Joyce actually wrote). Penelope cannot escape the contents of her myth for she does not exist except in relation to them, and any change in her character will ripple throughout the myth.

We can now restate the correlation between a myth and language as the myth's ability to bring to a text both denotative and connotative meanings and, when segmented, to yield both a "free" and a "bound" character. Through their study of a lexicon, linguists have shown that a language is a system as well as a set, that it is as much the *relations* among the parts as the parts themselves that compose the whole. For example, the "meaning" of a morpheme is determined not only by its signification but also by its function. *Un* is simply two letters or a grunt until we know its sense (negativity) and its valence (limited to the prefix position). It has value in isolation primarily because it has a history of associations; separated from its counterparts, *un* openly reflects the essence of those meetings. As we have seen, literary and scholarly practices have caused myth, too, to become concurrently segregated and integrated, its parts independent and dependent. The best overview of this dual nature of both myth and language comes in Ernst Cassirer's formulation of "mythico-linguistic" thought: "Every part of a whole is the whole itself; every specimen is equivalent to the entire species. The part does not merely represent the whole, or the specimen its class; they are identical with the totality to which they belong; not merely as mediating aids to reflective thought, but as genuine presences which actually contain the power, significance and efficacy of the whole."[22]

The Grammar of Myth

Given the several semiotic characteristics of a myth's fragments, it seems useful to designate them—upon analogy to the phonemes, morphemes, and sememes of linguistics—mythemes. Ideally we would find that the fragments formed by scholars and authors constituted a complete sign system, but even if we could collect every such myth segment for analysis, this coincidence is highly unlikely. Since we are concerned with a myth's disposition in fiction and not with its internal character or its distribution throughout mythology or anthropology, we need not be scrupulously exact in marking these mythemes. Nevertheless, for the purposes of consistency and comparison, we should analyze a myth coherently. It seems best to proceed deductively, choosing a classifying principle that creates an efficient, productive, inclusive system.

This move is not without precedent. Structuralist critics in particular have attempted to construct grammars of narrative with schemes designed by Roland Barthes, Julia Kristeva, Tzvetan Todorov, and A. J. Greimas, to name only the most well known.[23] In regard to myth (although in a different context and to different ends), Claude Lévi-Strauss' "A Structural Study of Myth" provides a substantial effort at delineating such a grammar. The approach of Lévi-Strauss has been extensively critiqued; yet despite undeniable weaknesses in his methodology,[24] his example still furnishes a valuable taxonomy for anyone interested in distilling a myth to its essential elements, for whatever reasons.

In his famous essay, Lévi-Strauss assumes that myths can be treated the same way that linguists treat words. Because a myth *is* language (to be known it must be told), he contends that it, too, is composed of "gross constituent units," which he calls mythemes. But because a myth is also *other* than language (we do not confuse it with other forms of human speech since it performs at a high level "where meaning succeeds practically at 'taking off' from the linguistic ground on which it keeps on rolling"), he surmises that the mytheme is found at the sentence level.[25] To illustrate his formula, Lévi-Strauss divides the Oedipus myth into eight principal and three subsidiary mythemes. The former units are short sentences describing "relations," such as "Oedipus kills his father, Laios"; the three latter ones are simply etymological equations, such as "Oedipus = swollen-foot." Except for the fact that only four of these eleven mythemes deal directly with Oedipus' life—the rest concern the origins of Thebes and the actions of Oedipus' children—they might be mistaken for the motif or thematic subdivisions of other scholars who have studied Oedipus' history.[26]

Yet the great difference between Lévi-Strauss' construction of his mythemes and the classificatory systems of other critics lies in its parallel with linguistics. If nothing else, this analogy recognizes myth's fundamental communicative and organic character and provides terminology for reflecting that character. In other words, it is only superficially that mytheme seems synonymous with concept, theme, or motif. In reality, it is a more complex idea implying a network of associations and a reflexiveness that are endemic to myth but ignored by these other terms. The mytheme is, finally, a concept capable of suggesting, by its name alone, the reciprocal communication—from myth to text and from text to myth with the reader as decoder—that occurs when a myth appears in fiction.

But if Lévi-Strauss reveals the value of the mytheme, he does not provide an adequate methodology for constructing it. As a number of critics have pointed out, Lévi-Strauss' methods are willful, personal, and idiosyncratic.[27] Better guidance comes from Terence Turner, who uses the principles and techniques of structural linguistics and transformational grammar to show the failures of Lévi-Strauss' system and to formulate a more consistent and comprehensive approach to narrative analysis. As Turner observes, "The simplest unit of narrative is the act, that is, a meaningful act with an explicit or implicit purpose: in short, a social (human) act. Narrative is, in effect, an ordered sequence of action."[28] Turner's approach suggests that a grammar of narrative should be first of all a grammar of actions. The analyst must determine "which events, actions, or in general, relations, appear to depend directly upon one another for their meaning, and which are remotely related."[29]

Turner's method is not a panacea. For one thing, as Robert Scholes observes, many elements in myths and other tales are not functions of the narrative itself, yet they still play some fundamental role; they are semantic rather than syntactic in their working.[30] This reservation could explain why Lévi-Strauss includes the etymologies of Oedipus', Laius', and Labdacus' names in his scheme. However, as we will see in the next chapter, such semantic units usually play a signaling rather than a signifying role in modern fiction and consequently do not qualify as mythemes. Another problem with adopting Turner's scheme is that it focuses on narrative in general and thus ignores those properties unique to myth, mainly its intertextuality and openness to interpretation. However, this shortcoming is easily overcome by recalling an earlier observation: when we break up a myth into its component parts, we are also breaking up previous interpretations. Each mytheme inherently invokes these annotations so that it resembles a palimpsest, with layers of meaning that resonate through to the mytheme's surface.

A final problem with Turner's approach is not so quickly surmounted, since it is one that every analyst of narrative must face—or ignore: the inability to eliminate subjectivity and arbitrariness when dividing up the story. Deciding which actions "depend directly upon one another for their meaning" requires that the analyst *interpret* the narrative, that is, select a particular way to view it that privileges some actions over others. In addition, as Alan Dundes notes in describing the minimal units of the proverb, "the critical question of precisely where to make one's 'cuts', that is, where to subdivide what may well be a continuum, is not easy to settle and the answer as often as not is admittedly somewhat arbitrary. In theory, one can always divide any proposed minimal unit into still smaller units."[31]

While I cannot completely eliminate subjectivity and arbitrariness, I can perhaps minimize those qualities by being aware of them and by checking my analysis against the divisions of others, those of imaginative writers as well as those of analysts.[32] Indeed, in order to retain one of the essential qualities of myth, its susceptibility—even its invitation—to interpretation, the mytheme should be expressed as neutrally as possible. For example, "Oedipus blinds himself in despair" would not be a proper mytheme because it restricts interpretation instead of welcoming it.

Keeping in mind the several limitations of this methodology, I propose that Sophocles' version of the Oedipus myth comprises the following mythemes:

1. An oracle warns Laius that he will be murdered by a son born of him and his wife Jocasta.
2. The son's feet are fastened together, and he is given to a shepherd to leave in the Theban hills.
3. The shepherd disobeys the order and gives the baby to a fellow shepherd who delivers him to King Polybus and Queen Merope of Corinth.
4. The child, named Oedipus, grows up as the son of Polybus and Merope.
5. Inquiring about his parentage, Oedipus learns from the oracle that he is destined to kill his father and marry his mother.

6. Attempting to circumvent the oracle's prophecy, Oedipus leaves Corinth.
7. At a crossroads, Oedipus has a run-in with a man—who unknown to him is his father—and his attendants and murders them all.
8. Oedipus encounters the Sphinx at the gates of Thebes and answers her riddle, thus causing her suicide and saving the city.
9. Oedipus marries the widowed queen, Jocasta, who—unknown to both of them—is his mother.
10. Jocasta and Oedipus have four children—two sons and two daughters.
11. After reigning peacefully for many years, Oedipus must deal with a plague that infects Thebes.
12. The oracle relates that the unpunished murderer of Laius is the cause of the plague.
13. Oedipus initiates an investigation to find the person who killed Laius.
14. Informed of the death of Polybus and of his real relationship to this king, Oedipus begins to seek his origins.
15. Oedipus simultaneously discovers the truth of his past and that he is the criminal he seeks.
16. Oedipus' mother-wife, Jocasta, commits suicide.
17. Oedipus blinds himself with Jocasta's brooches.
18. Oedipus is exiled from Thebes and cared for by his daughter Antigone.
19. Oedipus becomes favored by the gods, so that good fortune comes to those who protect him and suffering to those who threaten him.
20. Oedipus refuses to help either of his sons, who are fighting for the throne of Thebes, and in fact curses them to death.
21. Befriended by Theseus, Oedipus dies in a mysterious way outside Athens, in Colonus.

Undoubtedly, arguments can be made about this list. Depending upon the analyst's evaluation of actions that are crucial to Oedipus' story, the group could be expanded, reduced, or revised. For example, I can envision someone wanting to include a mytheme about Jocasta's attempt to keep Oedipus from pursuing his interrogation. Further, in compiling this set I have had to resolve some inconsistencies among Sophocles' three plays, most notably the revelation in *Antigone* that Oedipus died soon after his self-mutilation. But while I anticipate dissent on some points, I believe most readers will agree that each of these twenty-one mythemes is integral to Sophocles' presentation of Oedipus and that, taken together, they constitute the shape and substance of Oedipus' life. If nothing else, perhaps readers will allow that this system satisfies the needs of this study and can be productive within that context. In the following chapter I explore how these mythemes enable us to schematize the experience of reading and interpreting twentieth-century fiction that, in some fashion, uses the Oedipus myth.

C H A P T E R   2

A Poetics for Myth in Fiction

■

As Eric Gould notes, the process of reading fiction that uses myth has been most often described as the activity of "fitting together motifs and archetypes into a solution to a giant puzzle" (140). To put this another way, many critics have assumed that myth criticism consists of translation, with myth serving as the master text by which we decode the modern text. John White has recently attempted to correct this simplistic view by proposing that the mythological novel employs myth as prefiguration. But while this approach appears to consider things from the reader's perspective, it still misses much of the reader's activity. The problem with White's account is the same problem that Wolfgang Iser finds in the idea of *rezeptionsvorgabe* (structured prefigurement), which is used by German academics to describe any text: "Of course, the text is a 'structured prefigurement', but that which is given has to be received, and the *way* in which it is received depends as much on the reader as on the text."[1]

If myth functions like a language inside the bounds of fiction, a language highly charged with meaning and ambiguity, then readers who attend to it are not translators or simple reactors. Rather, they are participants in a dialogue—a dialogue involving numerous texts and that is, finally, interminable. In this chapter I explore the intricacies of the reading process in detail, but to anticipate the central role of the reader, we need recall only that signs do not automatically *mean*, but rather they ask that meaning be found for them. As Umberto Eco observes, "The understanding of signs is not a mere matter of recognition (of a stable equivalence); it is a matter of *interpretation*."[2] This emphasis on the reader, prescribed by semiotics, also aligns my perspective with that of reader-centered critics

15

who maintain that the literary work is situated somewhere between the author's text and the reader's realization of that text. According to Iser, one of this group's most influential exponents, "In literary works . . . the message is transmitted in two ways, in that the reader 'receives' it by composing it."[3] By substituting "signs" for "literary works" in this sentence we can see the similarity between the signification process discussed by the semiotician and the actualization process studied by the reader-response critic.

A myth thus lies dormant in a narrative until a reader makes it dynamic, a process that begins with an act of recognition. Obviously, the readers I am referring to throughout this study are those who are interested in myth and who are prepared to recognize it.[4] Such readers become aware of a myth by one of three means: (1) the text refers to the myth or part of it; (2) the text explicitly introduces a mytheme; or (3) the text implicitly presents a mytheme. Not only are these the means by which readers first perceive a myth, but they are also the ways in which they subsequently receive it. Alone and in combination, these three categories form the continuum suggested by the phrase "myth in fiction."

Traditionally, critics have reserved the terms *mythic* or *mythological* for fiction in which explicit references to the myth (categories 1 and/or 2) make substantial appearances in conjunction with implied mythemes (category 3).[5] But if we determine that the reader as much as the author produces the literary text, then the fact of authorial intention changes primarily the reading experience, not our final assessment of the myth's role. To put this another way, we can say that a story possesses a mythological component so long as the myth, regardless of whether implicitly or explicitly presented, significantly influences our actualization of the work and thereby serves as one of the work's ordering structures. When this criterion is met, the main reason for distinguishing explicit references to the myth from implicit references is that they evoke different reading experiences. When writers make a point of naming a myth, they are deliberately manipulating our response. Actualizing this type of narrative will thus differ from actualizing a story where we discern the myth without the author's direct "intervention."

16

This is not to say that readers should—or will—ignore the author's intentions for using myth. Because semiosis is interminable,[6] it makes sense to start with the author's guidance, to be concerned with the way in which the author sets up relationships between a myth and the text. To use Peter Rabinowitz' terms, we should first become members of the "authorial audience"—the particular social/interpretive community that the author wrote for[7]—and try to understand the myth within that context. But because each mytheme possesses an extensive semantic encyclopedia—an encyclopedia that continues to grow rather than diminish—we should also be prepared to move beyond the authorial reading and, in Terry Eagleton's words, "show the text as it cannot know itself."[8] I would even argue that such a movement falls under the heading of an "intentionalist reading," since, by its very nature, myth invites us to negotiate texts, to initiate a dialogue between itself and the modern narrative. In effect, the author who, consciously or unconsciously, introduces myth into the text gives us license to pursue semiosis for as long as we wish—but at least until that dialogue has been accomplished.

The Mythic Signal

The first way readers can become aware of a myth is when the text (or, if one prefers, the author) briefly alludes to it. This kind of reference is like a signal; it tells us nothing—or very little—*about* the myth but merely hints that we might find additional evidence of it elsewhere in the story. At one time in the history of the prose narrative such a citation did not imply that the myth would reappear. Before the twentieth century, writers frequently used myth to highlight their themes. For example, George Eliot could write in *The Mill on the Floss* (1860) that "Mr. Tulliver had a destiny as well as Oedipus, and in this case he might plead, like Oedipus, that his deed was inflicted on him rather than committed by him"[9] without further applying Oedipus' story to hers. Victorian readers would have regarded the simile as a means of insight into the character and circumstances of Mr. Tulliver but would not have expected the parallel to spread throughout the text. However, with the fiction of James Joyce, D. H. Lawrence, Thomas Mann, and other early modernists, myth became a method as well as a metaphor[10]; and we have learned that a reference to a myth often reaches far beyond the page where we find it, although it need not.[11]

The several guises that mythic allusions can take have been thoroughly cataloged by White. He lists titles, epigraphs, quotations, figures of speech, chapter headings, character names, and mythic scenery, such as statues, paintings, and tapestries. In regard to the Oedipus myth, we find examples of an author signaling the myth's presence in titles such as *Oedipus Burning*, "Oedipus-Schmoedipus," "My Oedipus Complex," and "The Way to Colonus"; in Alain Robbe-Grillet's epigraph to *The Erasers*, modified slightly from Sophocles' *Oedipus the King* ("Time that sees all has found you out against your will"); and in the name of Thomas Pynchon's protagonist in *The Crying of Lot 49*, Oedipa Maas, and of David Lang's central character in *Oedipus Burning*, Odie Spangler.

As White observes, when these clues come early in the story, often in the prefatory material (as titles and epigraphs must), they function prefiguratively. We see them as a promise that the plot will follow "a whole configuration of actions or figures" found in the myth.[12] But to repeat my earlier observation, the notion of prefiguration fails to do full justice to the reader's role as structuring agent. Another problem with this term is that it cannot accurately reflect the reader's response when the mythic reference comes later in a story, after the title page and preface, as it so often does, sometimes even coming near the story's end.[13] White briefly admits that a late reference to a myth can occur, and he even has a name for such a tardy allusion: the "delayed-action prefiguration."[14] But the contradictory quality of this label reveals that White is stretching to make the idea of prefiguration cover all cases. In truth, when the reference appears anywhere beyond the story's opening page, it requires some mental acrobatics, asking that readers turn Janus-like and search the text in both directions—reexamining what we have read and watching the plot closely as we continue to read—for additional evidence of the myth. As Peter Brooks notes in his discussion of narrative in general, "Causation can work backward as well as forward since the effect of event, or of phantasy, often comes only when it takes on meaning . . . which may occur with considerable delay. . . . Thus the way a story is ordered does not necessarily correspond to the way it *works*."[15] In general, the thing to remember about mythic allusions is that they are like stage directions; they set us in motion but demand a larger background—that is, an assemblage of mythemes—against which their cues will make sense.

The Explicit Mytheme as Signal and Sign

The second way readers can apprehend a myth's presence is through an explicit mytheme. This method is similar to the first in that the myth is named, either by the narrator or by a character, thereby urging us to look both behind and ahead in our reading for other indications of it. But this time, instead of a brief allusion to the myth, we are introduced, usually at some length, to one or more mythemes. For instance, in Michel Butor's *Passing Time*, George Burton, the author of a popular murder mystery, tells the narrator, Jacques Revel,

> "The detective is a true son of the murderer Oedipus, not only because he solves a riddle, but also because he kills the man to whom he owes his title, without whom he would not exist in that capacity (without crimes, without mysterious crimes, what would he be?) because this murder was foretold for him from the day of his birth or, if you prefer, because it is inherent in his nature, through it alone he fulfils [sic] himself and attains the highest power."[16]

This is the first passage in which Oedipus is specifically mentioned, and it presents us with at least three Oedipal mythemes: Oedipus as fated (5); Oedipus as murderer (7); and Oedipus as riddle solver (8). Similar to a mythic allusion, all these mythemes advertise the possibility that the myth might provide structural and substantive keys to the story. However, the big difference between these explicit mythemes and the mythic signals previously discussed is that the mythemes directly guide our effort to confirm the narrative's mythic dimension. Butor's character has given us specific instructions about which Oedipal mythemes (actions/episodes) to look for in the narrative. If we find that this trio of mythemes (and/or others) implicitly shapes the story, then we will have confirmed our suspicion that the explicit mythemes are important: we are now able to explain the action of the novel in terms of the explicit mythemes.

Justifying the explicit mytheme with the implicit marks the true beginning of the process of signification. In other words, this justification amounts to recognizing a sign and is thus similar to a driver's arrival at a traffic light or a reader's encounter with a word; in all cases, awareness of the sign creates the need for interpretation. A brief review of this signification process will help to clarify the response that the implicit mytheme evokes from readers.

Most semioticians assume that a sign consists of an action between pairs: the expression (the signifier), which we perceive, and the content (the signified or the concept), which we infer.[17] A red light, for instance, becomes the expression that means stop to a driver. Of course, what we infer depends upon context. When the red light that caused the driver to brake is put in a city window, it could mean that the house is a brothel or is decorated for Christmas. Precedent also plays a part in inference drawing. Because lawmakers at one time decided that a red light at an intersection would signify stop and because custom has decreed that a red light in a window announces sexual activity, the red light means these things to someone traveling in the city today. A red light in the woods will baffle or amuse its observer, who needs more information before making any inferences. But that does not mean that this red light cannot become a sign. A hiker might see in it a sign of distress or warning; a conceptual artist, a sign of creativity. The point of this example is to show just how much contextual information is embedded in a statement like "a red light means stop." Linguistic signs work similarly. To cite an example popular among rhetoricians and linguists, "Fire!" signifies a disaster to patrons of a theatre and an order to pull a trigger to a firing squad. Again, context and precedent inform content.

As these samples make clear, the meaning of a sign is not merely a matter of recognition (this sign = this meaning), but results from an interpretation (this sign = this meaning in this situation). To quote Eco again, "The sign is an instruction for interpretation, a mechanism which starts from an initial stimulus and leads to all its illative consequences" (26). Indeed, many semioticians, including Eco, deny that a set equivalence of sign and meaning ever exists, except for pragmatic reasons. Even when the rule for inference seems automatic—as it might for the driver facing the traffic light who essentially recalls a law—Eco argues that the individual has "*to decide* to connect that Rule with that Result through the mediation of the Case" (41). He labels this type of automatic or quasi-automatic inference a "hypothesis" or an "overcoded abduction"—abduction being "the tentative and hazardous tracing of a system of signification rules which will allow the sign to acquire its meaning" (40).[18]

Eco describes two other kinds of abduction, undercoded and creative. In the former type, the decoder must select a rule from a series of equally probable alternatives. For instance, when someone says, "this is a man," we must decide whether that person means this is a rational animal, a mortal creature, a good specimen of virility, or something else. Contextual and circumstantial clues might indicate which meaning is the most plausible, but we cannot be certain whether it is the most correct or the only correct meaning until we can further test the case. In contrast to undercoded abduction, creative abduction occurs when the decoder must invent *ex novo* the rule acting as an explanation (42), as did the observers of the red light in the woods in the example discussed above. Eco illustrates this type of abduction by referring to Copernicus' intuition that the world is heliocentric and to the interpretations of many symbols. As he concludes, in creative abductions, no preexisting explanation exists, as it does for over-and undercoded abductions, and so one cannot be positive that he or she has interpreted the sign reasonably (42–43).

Eco's taxonomy can help establish the various ways that readers (who replace the driver as the decoder of the sign) might respond to a mytheme (the red light's proxy) in a text (substituting for the city street). Simply because myths are polysemantic and because twentieth-century authors change mythic stories to fit their own, readers, unlike drivers, will probably never engage in an overcoded abduction. However, since each mytheme appropriates every inter-pretation formally proposed for it, we could *almost* automatically apply one of the explanations to the mytheme(s) at hand. In regard to the Oedipus myth, the incest and patricide mythemes are the most likely candidates, especially when found together, to provoke such a quick response, for Freud's reading of these signs has almost totally prescripted them. Yet I hesitate to call even such an "instant" association overcoded since readers will still need to verify this choice with textual and extratextual evidence and possibly other mythemes.

As the rule-making activity of signification, abduction applies to our meeting with any implicit mytheme marked in the text, regard-less of whether we are directed to this mytheme by its explicit counterpart; and so we have moved beyond the goal of describing how readers respond to the first explicit mytheme(s) of a story. However, because undercoded and creative abductions must include in their operations the entire text and its mythemes, an initial myth-eme could hardly be analyzed in isolation. This is not to suggest that the earliest mytheme, or any mytheme, refuses interpretation within its immediate context. I merely repeat that readers will only tenta-tively formulate a meaning until finishing the story. In fact, the reading and rereading of a narrative using the Oedipus myth might be compared to Oedipus' own development. Upon a first reading, we are like the Oedipus of *Oedipus the King*, understanding imperfectly, collecting and registering signs, but having to wait until the story's end for a full understanding of them. With each subsequent reading, we possess at least some of the inner vision of the Oedipus in *Oedipus at Colonus*; each mytheme makes more sense and even illuminates details missed the first time.

The best way to see how the various kinds of abduction describe our meeting with a mytheme is to trace these interpretive processes in regard to specific texts. To bridge that undertaking with the preceding discussion, figure 1 illustrates at a glance the several sources feeding our abduction. The mytheme is shaded, because it

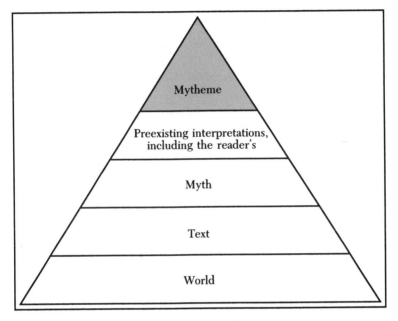

Figure 1. Sources for Mythemic Abduction in Fiction

is our awareness of this sign that initiates the search for meaning. We are, of course, constantly considering all areas depicted in the figure, and thus none supersedes or precludes the others, although there will be times—especially after the story has been read, as we attempt to consolidate and confirm an interpretation—when we will consciously seek out one over the rest. Hence, in ordering these fields within this discussion, I am making sequential and deliberate a process that is in reality somewhat vague and chaotic.

In considering this figure, we must also recognize that the search for meaning will be influenced—as it is for any narrative element, not just for myth—upon the *source* of the mytheme and its manner of presentation. Because most twentieth-century fiction has done away with the intrusive narrator, like that of George Eliot's *The Mill on the Floss*, who draws comparisons between the world of the text and a past world, explicit mythemes almost always originate with a character. How closely that character applies these signs to his or her situation will dictate the amount and kind of interpretive labor that readers subsequently undertake. When the character consciously draws parallels between his or her position and that of a mythic figure, our work will include testing the character's reliability. When a character is less percipient or totally unaware of such parallels, we will be absorbed with substantiating our own extension of the myth into the story. To state this business more generally, in either case we are concerned with determining the function of the mytheme, be it to express irony, to serve as a heuristic device, to parody mythological parallels, or to perform some other role.

As an example of the reader's attempt to verify an identification, we can take another look at the passage from *Passing Time* previously referred to. Here George Burton does not directly apply the three Oedipal mythemes to his or Revel's circumstances; and so, on the one hand, we might view this analogy as simply Burton's poetic explanation of the mechanics of the detective story. On the other hand, because Revel's own narrative, a diary of his year in Bleston, has itself started to take the form of a detective story, many readers will, as I have suggested, see the Oedipus myth as a potential informer of Revel's life; they will therefore seek the implicit mythemes that would support this hypothesis.[19]

The most common way that an explicit mytheme is introduced into a modern story is through a character who draws direct comparisons between his or her life and that of a mythic hero. Such self-conscious paralleling always runs the risk of typing the character as pretentious or excessive; and perhaps the most difficult problem for the author who chooses this method is to make such analogizing seem sufficiently motivated, not contrived.[20] The better writers, such as Butor and Alberto Moravia, succeed at this; and once we grant the character

24

his or her right to poetic license, these analogies can indicate far more important personality traits than pedantry. The mythemes become, in effect, a sort of waking dream by which we can analyze that character as well as a potentially plausible correspondence that will shed light on both the story and the myth. One of the best examples of this type of mythic presentation comes in Moravia's *The Lie*. In order to illustrate the kind of participation demanded from readers of such narratives, I will spend some time tracing this involvement, focusing especially upon the process of signification, which constitutes the most important part of this involvement and about which this chapter is primarily concerned.

Sixty pages into this 330-page novel, Francesco Merighi, the story's narrator, tells us that he has awakened from a nightmare in which his wife, Cora, was the procuress of himself and his stepdaughter, Baba. To calm himself, he turned on the light and picked up a book, which happened to be *Oedipus the King*. After reading the first few pages, Francesco wept, because

> I found myself in the same situation as Oedipus: the city tainted by plague was my family, which was also tainted; and I, like Oedipus, had questioned all the witnesses to find out who was the cause of this corruption and had discovered that the one who bore the guilt of the corruption was myself. But here—and now my thoughts began to be confused by returning sleep—here the resemblance ended. For to Oedipus it had been granted to pluck out his eyes, to transfer his guilt by means of a rite, to free himself from it by changing evil into good. But I? I had to content myself with knowing, beyond any doubt, that I myself was to blame for the corruption, even if in a remote and indirect way; but I could do nothing: I could neither punish myself nor make any expiation, nor transform what was negative into something positive. Unless . . . upon this "unless," in which there seemed to be a glimmer of hope, I fell asleep.[21]

This passage, the first in which Francesco directly refers to the Oedipus myth, introduces four Oedipal mythemes: Oedipus confronting a plague after a number of peaceful years as ruler (11);

Oedipus leading an investigation to eliminate the cause of the plague (13); Oedipus tracking down the contagium as himself (15); and Oedipus blinding himself (16). As I have indicated, one of our first acts as readers will be to assess the justness of Francesco's analogy by seeking the implicit functioning of these explicit mythemes. Because we do not yet know much about Francesco or his history, we cannot immediately complete this search; it will, consequently, engage us throughout our reading of this novel.

However, we can at this point form some preliminary assumptions that will guide that search, the most important ones arising from the changes Francesco has made in these mythemes. For one, he has substituted his family for the city of Thebes. He thus reduces the range of the corruption, eliminating its sociopolitical aspect.[22] When we ask how Francesco has caused his family's corruption and in what way Cora and Baba are "diseased," we find very little to go on except the vague notion that he believes his ten-year withdrawal from family life somehow pushed Cora into prostitution. This inference is confirmed several pages later when Francesco states: "I was directly responsible for the profession practiced by Cora, inasmuch as, by ceasing to love her and parting from her, I had destroyed all desire in her for a regular family life and had thus driven her toward her secret vocation" (83). In brief, whereas the Theban plague resulted from crimes Oedipus committed, the corruption of Francesco's family has arisen from acts Francesco has refused to perform. Another change Francesco makes in comparing himself to Oedipus is that he resists, at least for the moment, applying the self-blinding mytheme to his situation, first by regretting that Oedipus' recourse is not open to him and then by suggesting that he may be able to entirely avoid self-punishment by acting on his self-knowledge and by containing, perhaps even curing, the corruption he is responsible for. In other words, Francesco claims that he possesses Oedipus' inner sight but need not suffer the physical sign of that possession: his story will begin *before* the denouement of *Oedipus the King* and, he implies, will describe how he restores his family to health.

In creating these expectations for the novel's future action, we see how White's idea of prefiguration might pertain. But as we continue to read *The Lie*, composed primarily of entries from Francesco's diary, we discover that most of these initial inferences are wrong. Francesco has misled us, not necessarily deliberately, for he actually has *not* faced up to his past when his story begins. He has indeed repressed, or suppressed, its most incriminating moment: his meeting six years earlier with Baba, arranged by Cora as a sexual rendezvous but aborted when Francesco fled (and thus we learn that Francesco's nightmare was based in reality). Consequently, the explicit mythemes that Francesco suggests have already functioned in his life—Oedipus' investigation and ensuing recognition—turn out to be the mythemes implicitly controlling the story. As in *Oedipus the King*, the major action of *The Lie* consists of the protagonist questioning various witnesses and growing to awareness; thus, as we follow a man who confronts, bit by bit, the truth about his past, our experience as readers ends up closely duplicating that of an audience watching Sophocles' drama for the first time. Of course, Moravia's novel goes one step beyond Sophocles' tragedy when Francesco complicates his anagnorisis by giving us two contradictory conclusions regarding the history of his relationship with Baba and his knowledge of Cora's profession. Francesco's unreliability as narrator keeps the self-blinding mytheme suspended when the novel ends (we never know whether his guilt and self-blame are sincere), unless we accept his view that both endings are true in their own way, in which case truth and guilt become relative.

By searching for implicit mythemes to validate, or invalidate, the explicit mythemes introduced by Francesco, we have moved ahead in our reading. Let us return, then, to that first lengthy Oedipal analogy and look at other acts of the abductive process precipitated by these mythemes. At the same time that we are using explicit mythemes to anticipate the plot and to elucidate Francesco's character, we are also reviewing pages already read for other signs of the myth. In particular, most readers will, I believe, link Francesco's thoughts of committing incest with his stepdaughter (described by Francesco several pages before his dream and evidently a catalyst for his comparison with Oedipus) to Oedipus' marriage to Jocasta (mytheme 9). Our connection of Francesco's incestuous feelings to

27

Oedipus' situation provides an example of a purely implicit mytheme (that is, the text did not explicitly introduce it) and illustrates how each mytheme invokes all others. In fact, simply on the strength of this implicit mytheme, many readers might have associated Francesco with Oedipus *before* Francesco himself drew the parallel and could thus have been awaiting additional mythemes to confirm this supposition. However, in making this connection we must deal with the fact that, once again, the expression of an Oedipal mytheme has changed. Stepfather and stepdaughter have replaced son and mother, just as the family supplanted the city and non-deeds took the place of deeds.

Permutations in a mytheme's expression open up, to an even greater degree than usual, the question of its meaning. Shifts in the signifier create gaps in the signified, although every mytheme seems protean to the extent that it can absorb variation in its expression without suffering an identity crisis. All signs accommodate a certain amount of change without losing their character. For example, many shades of red will cause a driver to stop; indeed, like most semiotic systems, this one functions by difference and by relationship so that anything not yellow or green in the "red" position is likely to be interpreted as red. Similarly, different pronunciations of a word or variant spellings (the British *centre* versus the American *center*) still refer to the same concept. In sum, the expression of every sign has an invariable core, but also a modifiable periphery—a periphery whose limits we are constantly testing with mispronunciations, misspellings, and other misformations.

It is, in fact, within the mytheme's permutations that the exchange between myth and text reaches its most lively state. As Francesco describes this revision: "I was searching for the truth—not so much about Oedipus as about myself; and it was therefore right that I should make use of the tragedy solely for a better understanding of the situation in which I found myself" (82–83). Eric Gould expresses this rationale from the position of the twentieth-century author: "There seems a limited future in self-consciously repeating the great classical tales we have inherited and reworked for some centuries now without allowing their progress into the modern" (125). In

28

gauging this "progress into the modern," readers find new meaning in the myth as well as understanding for the modern story. In brief, then, an inference made for an altered mytheme will include an extra step of measurement not needed in the abductive process for an intact mytheme.

For instance, in the incest mytheme of *The Lie*, the exchange of stepfather-stepdaughter for son-mother does not seem all that unusual since we are familiar with the psychoanalytic practice of plugging different family members into the original Oedipal constellation or emphasizing different tensions among these members and then locating a myth that represents these changes: for example, the Electra complex (the daughter's attraction to her father); the Atreus or Heracles complex (the father's hatred of his children); the Orestes complex (the son's hatred of his mother); and the Medea complex (the mother's hatred of her daughter).[23] Recently it has even been proposed that love of a stepparent for a stepchild be designated the Phaedra complex,[24] an assignation that could call into question which myth best informs Francesco's love for Baba. Nevertheless, for several reasons, not the least of which is that Francesco himself has chosen the Oedipus myth as a prototype for his situation, we should finally see the incest mytheme of *The Lie* as an altered Oedipal mytheme rather than as a mytheme from another myth.

Indeed, from one angle we can view this revision as simply a rectifying of the Oedipal incest mytheme as interpreted by Freud, since father-daughter liaisons are far more prevalent in our patriarchal society (as they were in ancient Greece) than mother-son relationships.[25] Francesco modernizes the incest mytheme in yet another way: his explanation of his desire for Baba draws upon the discoveries of some twentieth-century biologists that humans are naturally incest averse and upon the suggestions of sociopsychologists that the taboo is cultural and ideological.[26] As he observes, "I became aware that, if it had not been for the idea, or rather the name, of incest, I should probably not have desired her" (56). But in this admission we find the major change in the incest mytheme: unlike Oedipus, Francesco is consciously aware of the prohibition against his attraction to Baba *at the time* that he pursues her. More important, this prohibition *creates* his desire, so much so that he must imagine incest where none literally exists. Whereas Oedipus' discovery of his true relationship to Jocasta horrified and repulsed him and led to his self-mutilation, Francesco needs blood ties in order to feel anything at all for Baba.

In this need we get our first inkling that Francesco is a man obsessed by desire for the debased object, a preference of men that Freud first outlined in "A Special Type of Choice of Object Made by Men" (1910), significantly the paper in which he also first used the term *Oedipus complex*.[27] Francesco's love for Baba, as we discover later in the novel, is the latest, and most extreme, manifestation of this obsession; indeed, he sees incest as an attraction to nothingness (274, 302). This obsession originally revealed itself with Francesco's desire for Cora, a lower-class woman whom Francesco loved passionately until she began to display the effects of her upper-class married life (clean clothes, a stable home life, lovemaking in societally approved places). As Cora's social standing improved, Francesco's love waned, until he could find satisfaction only with prostitutes, who were sent to him secretly by Cora. Freud explains this type of desire as an improper "confluence of the affectionate and sensual currents," in which the man has been unable to surmount his respect for his first love object, his mother, and to see her also as a sexual being. As this description suggests and as several psychoanalysts working in a feminist tradition, notably Nancy Chodorow and Christiane Olivier, have shown, the very dynamics of parenting in a patriarchal culture make it difficult for many men to fuse properly these two currents.[28] Francesco is thus simply an extreme case of the typical man, or, perhaps, simply more honest.

But if Francesco's desire is at least partly impressed upon him by a patriarchal society, such a desire meets its nemesis in Baba's sociological defense against incest. Even though she seems attracted to Francesco and sometimes treats him ambiguously, Baba pressures Francesco to assume the role of father, not lover, and in this she instinctively recognizes that a breakdown of the formal family causes confusion of one's own identity. James Twitchell describes this requirement for the solidity of family roles:

Within each family there are in reality two families: one is formal, created by function, and the other is experiential, formed around feelings. There are male and female roles, and there are mother and father roles. To be successful a family needs to avoid any threat to these roles, not to deny pleasure, but to ensure cohesion. If this means the repression of the erotically experiential family, then so be it. The regulation of choices thus leads to the establishment and continual reaffirmation of, first, individual roles (father-daughter is not man-woman, but husband-wife is), then of families and finally of societies. Kinship is not biological; it is learned, and the impetus to learn the social structure is the prohibition on incest.[29]

Baba's effort to make Francesco learn kinship would keep him from becoming a full-fledged Oedipus. As Peter Rudnytsky states, "The result of Oedipus' incest is that time is frozen and each of his kinship ties *must have two names*"[30]; and Edward Said illustrates this idea similarly when he notes that "what overwhelms Oedipus is the burden of identities incapable of coexisting within one person."[31] Ironically, but inevitably, Baba's insistence on father-daughter roles merely intensifies Francesco's attraction that originates in such roles. Only when Baba marries does her plan triumph over Francesco's desire, for this act reinforces the father-daughter relationship while simultaneously eliminating the man-woman one.

This search for the meaning of the incest mytheme of *The Lie* has taken us through Freud to more recent theories about the psychological and sociological motivation of the incest taboo. And at first glance, it might also seem to have taken us away from Oedipus, who, in radical contrast to Francesco, tries to avoid incest and is horrified to learn that he has committed it. In fact, though, Francesco brings us back to Oedipus in his second lengthy analysis of the myth in which he describes *Oedipus the King* as a tragedy of noninvolvement. Oedipus' investigation, Francesco declares, teaches him to see himself and to see "how and why non-involvement took the place of involvement in his mind." Oedipus sees, in short, that "his crime

31

consisted not so much in succumbing to certain passions as in deluding himself into thinking he did not feel them and in making use of this delusion to give vent to them with impunity" (82). In this assessment of Oedipus, which is basically an interpretation of the self-incrimination mytheme (15), Francesco describes the mechanism of the human mind that enables one to repress crucial knowledge.[32] Yet, Francesco decides, "In interpreting the tragedy of Oedipus in this way," he is reducing the myth "to a psychological and subservient level" (82).

While many classical scholars would agree with Francesco that he is not justified in speculating about Oedipus' psychology,[33] such an approach has been popular in the commentary on *Oedipus the King* since at least the eighteenth century. A major question has been how Oedipus, considered the most intelligent of men, could fail to see the true nature of his situation. In fact, in *Sophocles and Oedipus*, Philip Vellacott advances an explanation of Sophocles' tragedy that is similar to Francesco's. According to Vellacott, "Sophocles shows us in a number of passages the sort of defence-system which Oedipus had built up for himself; a façade, a version of his story which made plausible sense, and which he trained himself and others to accept."[34]

Rudnytsky has recently modified this thesis, bringing it even closer to Francesco's interpretation, by replacing Vellacott's assumption of a deliberately self-incriminating Oedipus with the psychoanalytic tenet of unconscious knowledge. According to him, Oedipus' mistaken assumptions about his history can be regarded "in the manner of what Freud called the 'false connections' that go into the formation of neurotic symptoms, as a façade of self-delusion that is gradually destroyed by the analytic work of the play." For Oedipus, "the 'whole experience' of incest and patricide falls into an 'unconscious state,' and the prophecies of the oracle are thus the externalized projections of his own inadmissible desires."[35] Rudnytsky's analysis recalls also Jacques Lacan's reading of Oedipus as a man who always knows the answer but has repressed that knowledge. Oedipus moves, as any analysand must, from *méconnaissance* (a refusal or failure to recognize) to *reconnaissance* (recognition). Truth, in this case, is not knowledge (*savoir*) but recognition (*reconnaissance*).[36]

32

Whether or not we buy Francesco's interpretation of Oedipus' story—and the views of Vellacott, Rudnytsky, and Lacan suggest that such a reading is not eccentric—it does, as Francesco himself realizes, inform his psychology first. That is, Francesco has projected the facts of his life onto Oedipus' investigation, recognition, and self-blinding; and our main concern as readers must be to determine the significance of that projection for Moravia's novel. But this is not to say that Francesco has not introduced a plausible explanation of Oedipus' history that will encourage us to revise our understanding of the myth. Nor does it prevent us from assuming that Francesco's interpretation comments simultaneously upon a contemporary society that makes it possible, even desirable, for a person to remain uninvolved. As Hans Blumenberg observes, "Every reshaping [of a myth] will make clearer, as in an experiment, the operative forces that emerge from the present situation. [But concurrently, we] would know almost nothing of the significance of [a mythic figure] if this work on [myth] had not 'disclosed' it—or 'invented' it and superadded it."[37] Gould states that "we know that the Oedipus story, thanks to Greek Drama, Freud, and more recently, Claude Lévi-Strauss, is an important myth, telling us something about incest taboo, sexual identity crisis, kinship structures, and above all, suggests Lévi-Strauss, human origins" (183). Moravia, Vellacott, Rudnytsky, and Lacan reveal that we should add "the workings of the human mind" to this list.

This exploration of the abductive process related to the Oedipal mythemes of *The Lie* has certainly not treated all the complexities of this novel, but it has covered a great deal of that ground. To summarize briefly, we have seen that the explicit mythemes not only created expectations—finally overturned and replaced by other Oedipal patterns—for the novel's plot but also verified earlier suspicions about possible Oedipal associations. Our search for the meaning of the five active mythemes was slightly complicated by the fact that the content of these mythemes had, in most cases, been altered; however, we were able to resolve these gaps with information from the text, the myth's interpreters, and the fields of psychoanalysis and sociology. In Eco's terms, the abductive processes were both undercoded (previous explanations of the mythemes instructed our search in some cases) and creative (in most instances, our final interpretation was constructed through inferences that used Oedipus' commentators but did not rely solely upon them).

The Implicit Mytheme as Signal and Sign

In discussing the explicit mytheme we have also looked in detail at the implicit mytheme and how readers assign meaning to it. Despite this extensive description, we have yet to understand how readers recognize such a mytheme and how it can aid their actualization of a text when there is no explicit mythic signal or mytheme to initiate the search or to support the abduction. Obviously, recognition will depend to some degree upon familiarity. The better acquainted we are with a particular myth, the more likely we are to perceive mythemes from that myth, even when slightly revised. Familiarity, of course, breeds the danger of procrustean readings— one of the more serious charges brought against myth criticism— that is, of attempting to make the text fit the myth and vice versa, no matter what the damage done to the integrity of either. Avoiding such an accusation requires that we carefully verify both the mythemes and their significance in the narrative.

In general, we are prompted to see a specific myth as one of the text's ordering structures on two occasions: when we encounter "weighted" implicit mythemes or when we meet with a significant number of implicit mythemes. Weighted mythemes are those that, through the peculiarity of their expression or the publicity given them by one of the myth's interpreters, have a compelling ability to remind us of the myth. In the case of the Oedipus myth, the incest and patricide mythemes fall into this category, as might also the Sphinx and self-blinding mythemes. These last two merit this status because their unusual subject matter seems particular to the Oedipus myth; the first two have Freud to thank for their strength. But although a meeting with a weighted mytheme or with one that closely mimics its root can suggest the myth, it will take more than a brief, single encounter and, almost always, more than one mytheme

34

to convince readers that the myth has significance for the narrative. How many meetings and how many mythemes will depend upon the individual reader and the individual text, but a few examples will illustrate the range.

In some instances a weighted mytheme or mythemes will circulate so cogently throughout a narrative that the sheer momentum of the repeated image will turn readers to the myth. As one might expect, the incest mytheme alone or in conjunction with the patricide mytheme is frequently distributed and empowered in this way. In such cases, Freud's theories inevitably provide the departing point for the interpretation (more about this later, especially in chapter 5). D. H. Lawrence's *Sons and Lovers* has become one of the most famous examples of this implicit arrangement of the Freudian Oedipal mythemes, and its critical history emphasizes the predominant role that readers play in producing the literary work. Lawrence apparently conceived his novel without any firsthand acquaintance with Freud's theories about infant development. According to Frederick J. Hoffman, about the time that Lawrence was revising *Sons and Lovers* for publication, his wife, Freida, introduced him to Freud's work. Hoffman suggests that this introduction may have spurred Lawrence to highlight the mother-son relationship, but he warns, "The relationship was there long before Lawrence's final revision; and he did not allow any clinical or psychological commentary to interfere with the literary excellence of the novel as a whole."[38] That Freud played only a supporting role in Lawrence's composition of this book did not, however, prevent its first readers, especially psychoanalysts, from praising it as "the most penetrating study of the oedipus complex yet to be found in English literature."[39] The incest and patricide mythemes were simply too powerful to suppress such a reading, despite Lawrence's "intentions" or objections to the contrary.

This trend of reading *Sons and Lovers* from a Freudian position has continued to the present, although contemporary readers, under the influence of widespread Freudian revisionist movements, explain the incest and patricide mythemes very differently. For instance, Rosemary Davies, referring to Erich Fromm's theory that the child's incestuous relationship with the mother can be either life or death oriented, maintains that, counter to the traditional reading, the incest mytheme of Lawrence's novel fits the more destructive orientation. [40] In contrast, Giles Mitchell relies upon the psychoanalytic studies of Ernest Becker to reinterpret the Sphinx and oracle mythemes and then argues that the main instinct behind the Oedipus complex is fear of death, not incestuous desire. Mitchell contends that Paul Morel's story—and Oedipus'—depicts the struggle to come to terms with that fear, with one's own humanness. [41] In short, the critical history of *Sons and Lovers* reveals that changing assumptions about the world and the corresponding growth of a mytheme's semantic encyclopedia influence the meaning that readers find for that mytheme. To review the criticism of Lawrence's novel is to trace the evolution of psychoanalytic opinion (especially that concerning the two Oedipal mythemes that Freud adopted as cornerstones of his theory) and its application to literature.

A weighted implicit mytheme does not have to be used extensively in order to be noticed. It can receive such forceful emphasis in one part of a narrative that readers will be persuaded to view the myth as a vital source. For example, in Flannery O'Connor's *Wise Blood*, the main character, Haze Motes, blinds himself with lime, an act that represents his movement towards greater insight. "If there's no bottom in your eyes," he declares, "they hold more."[42] This self-blinding is the first time most readers will be urged to think of Oedipus, and it sets in motion the abductive process that involves examining the story for other Oedipal mythemes, reinserting this mytheme into the story line of the myth, accounting for the change in its expression (lime replaces the brooch as the instrument of self-mutilation), consulting previous interpretations of the mytheme for one that may apply, and determining function. Other Oedipal mythemes are certainly present: Haze's self-imposed exile from Eastrod (6); the strong hold that Mrs. Motes exerts over Haze's imagination and sexual experiences (9); and the suggestion that a destiny controls his life (5).

But the pivotal mytheme for O'Connor's novel is the self-blinding. It receives, as the others do not, the same thematic and structural emphases given it by the story line of the Oedipus myth. In other words, for both Oedipus and Haze, self-blinding is an act that resolves ironically a lifetime of not seeing what it was most necessary to see. O'Connor employs the other Oedipal mythemes only vaguely, changing their expressions and their placements in the sequence of events so that readers probably will *not* see them until the self-blinding mytheme opens their eyes. This ploy allows the self-blinding mytheme to surface suddenly, confronting readers with a recognition about the development of the story similar to the recognitions reached by Oedipus and Haze about the development of their lives. We are forced to return to the beginning of O'Connor's story and reassess Haze in light of this Oedipal configuration. A second reading of the story will darken his Oedipal outlines. We become more aware of the numerous ironic inversions associated with Oedipus' story: the seeing man who cannot see; the man who thinks he has all the answers who is himself in question; the savior who is the worst offender (O'Connor's novel is discussed in detail in chapter 5).

The other way that readers become aware of a myth is when they are overwhelmed by a number of implicit mythemes; in most cases of this kind, the mythemes assume approximately the same synchronic position in the character's life that they do in the mythic hero's life, and so readers grow gradually into awareness of the pattern being duplicated. These seem to have been the circumstances that led John Longley to see the life of William Faulkner's Joe Christmas in *Light in August* as a near repetition of Oedipus' history. In establishing the Oedipus-Christmas relationship, Longley points out the following: each man is ominously whisked away as an infant and raised by foster parents (mythemes 2 and 4), only to return later to the place where, unknown to him, he was born; each is responsible for his father's death (mytheme 7) and for the death of an older woman with whom he lives connubially (mytheme 16); and each man insists on defining himself and disregards alternative conduct that might be safer but would sidetrack this drive (mytheme 14).

Finally, each man meets a horrible ritual end—Oedipus in self-blinding and exile, Christmas in lynching and castration (mythemes 17 and 18). Longley concludes that, like Oedipus, Christmas has been "saddled with a terrible, inevitable curse. He did not ask for it and does nothing to deserve it; it was all 'decided' before he was born" (mythemes 1 and 5).[43] Although we might question various points of Longley's account of both Oedipus' and Christmas' stories—especially the idea that neither man does anything to deserve his fate[44]—this summary reveals that most of the Oedipal mythemes composing *Oedipus the King* are present in *Light in August* and form the substance of Christmas' life.

Because the expressions of many of these mythemes are modified, because they are spaced some distance from one another, and because the events they describe are chronologically scrambled, it is easy to understand why many readers miss seeing the Oedipus myth in *Light in August*. However, once the myth is pointed out, our interest turns towards apprehending how—or if—it helps to explain the action and characters of the novel. Faulkner himself admitted that Longley's analysis was justified, although he claimed not to have purposely used the Oedipus myth in constructing his story. "That's another matter of the writer reaching back into the lumber room of his memory for whatever he needs to create the character or the situation," he explained, "and the similarity is there but it was not by deliberate intent. It was by coincidence—not accident but by coincidence."[45]

Longley's study is the final product of the signification process evoked by implicitly presented mythemes. In his outline of Christmas' life, Longley interprets the relevant mythemes as they apply to both Oedipus and Christmas. In his conclusion he suggests that their final function is emotional, cathartic. According to him, in Christmas' lynching and castration—a version of the self-blinding mytheme—Faulkner has used

> the subconscious fear of mutilation and distrust of miscegenation that lurks in all of us, the love of and response to violence and death, the simultaneous love and hate of the loved one, to arouse these emotions or their equivalents in us. We love the violence and evil because we acquiesce in them. No doubt these emotions are despicable, but no doubt the emotions aroused by the spectacle of what Oedipus did were despicable also. The doctor who tamed

the legend of Oedipus and rechristened it a complex only found out very late what the Christian world had known all along: when there are guilt and filth in the human psyche, the only possible remedy is to cast them out.[46]

That another reader can interpret these mythemes differently—and even find other Oedipal mythemes in the text—is not the point or, rather, is exactly the point, since the thesis of these first two chapters has been that the principal quality of the mytheme is that it invites interpretation and is capable of spawning multiple meanings.[47] Much of the power of the mytheme resides in the fact that it takes us away from the story of the myth—to preexisting interpretations, to the world, and to other elements of the text—as much as it leads us to that story; it is, therefore, mistaken to think, as some critics have, that pairing the *events* of a myth with the events of a modern narrative constitutes a mythic approach.

As narrative structures, implicit mythemes, unlike explicit ones, stand on their own. Because they possess this autonomous nature, they can, finally, perform two other hermeneutic roles. First, by observing the way in which an author distributes these mythemes, either purposely or unconsciously, throughout his or her work, we can identify patterns that reveal artistic emphases or preoccupations. This kind of project is beyond the scope of this study, but one example will prove its feasibility. In an essay on Moravia written before publication of *The Lie*, Frank Baldanza argued that the structure of Moravia's *The Conformist, Ghost at Noon*, and *Conjugal Love* was essentially that of *Oedipus the King*. Baldanza asserted that in these novels, as in Sophocles' play, fate is "that set of irreparable circumstances and irresistible forces that is outside the cognizance of the central character." Thus the whole aesthetic structure of these three novels, as of Sophocles' tragedy, is "based on the rhythms of a movement toward anguished awareness of these forces."[48] This structure reappears, as Baldanza remarked in a second article on Moravia, in *The Lie*, where it is openly identified as Oedipal.[49] Baldanza's studies suggest that what I identify here as an implicit mytheme can disclose not only the concerns of a single work but also, when found throughout an author's fiction, the "fixations" of his or her imagination. By tracing such mythemes, critics might be able to understand better the whole of a writer's fictional output or its development.

The second intertextual role that the implicit mytheme can perform is to reveal the predilictions of an age or a culture. This scheme is identical to that just discussed except that we accomplish it by looking at how a group of authors uses the mythemes of a myth. As William Righter observes, "What we see depends upon what we are capable of seeing," and in most cases, we "see" myths "less as intrinsically 'there' than as the refracting lens through which our sensibility and its object interact."[50] By examining twentieth-century narratives that have used the Oedipus myth—noticing which Oedipal mythemes have been employed, how these mythemes have been altered, and how they have been distributed—we might be able, then, to learn something about what our society, at least the Western portion of it, is capable of seeing in Oedipus. This project is not beyond this study's scope and will be the focus of my last chapter. But such a project requires evidence, which the next three chapters will provide by investigating uses of the Oedipus myth in the three genres in which it most frequently—and almost exclusively—appears: science fiction, antidetective fiction, and psychological fiction.

C H A P T E R   3

The Power of the Solitary Mytheme:
The Anti-Sphinx of Alternative Wastelands

■

The claim that the mytheme possesses significant semiotic powers might be best supported by looking at the appearance of a single mytheme in a body of work. We find such a situation in the case of various science fiction narratives that have integrated into their plot lines the Sphinx mytheme from the Oedipus myth. By exploring the appearance of this mytheme in these several stories, we will be able to see more clearly how a mytheme can spur the imagination of both writers and readers. In addition, this exploration will also illustrate various other suggestions of the previous two chapters. For one, it will show that a mytheme never exists in true isolation, since we base our abduction of any mytheme partly on our understanding of its relationship to other mythemes of the myth. All the myth's mythemes are constantly present, whether in fact or in memory. Second, this investigation of the Sphinx mytheme in science fiction will illustrate the assumption that the semantic encyclopedia of a mytheme grows as much from our encounters with that mytheme in fiction as in scholarship. Our interpretation of the fictional renderings of a mytheme are as likely to inform our later meetings with that same mytheme as are our readings of critical exegesis.

Although the essence of science fiction has been frequently identified as mythic, critics have only recently started to recognize that the genre owes a long-standing debt to ancient mythologies. In the most comprehensive of these recent investigations, Casey Fredericks argues that Greek myths are particularly suited to the science fiction endeavor, since they reflect the rational and speculative concerns of the culture that produced them.[1] "In any case," Fredericks concludes, "Greek myths turn up everywhere in SF" (8). Fredericks' argument points to one reason why we might expect the Oedipus myth to appear in science fiction. As many classical scholars have shown, Oedipus evolved in ancient Greece into the paragon of the thinking man. Bernard Knox, for example, sees him as an extension of Periclean Athens itself, a prime representative of the intellectual quest of the age. As Knox puts it, "Oedipus investigates, examines, questions, infers; he uses intelligence, mind, thought; he knows, finds, reveals, makes clear, demonstrates; he learns and teaches; and his relationship to his fellow man is that of liberator and savior."[2] This character study of Oedipus seems very close to one we might construct for the scientist-explorer of science fiction. In brief, with his legendary intelligence and history of seeking answers, Oedipus was destined to attract the science fiction author.

Given that Oedipus' reputation as a truth seeker derives as much from his investigation into Laius' murder and into his own origins as it does from his answering of the Sphinx' riddle, it is somewhat surprising to find that only the Sphinx mytheme recurs in science fiction.[3] And yet, because that meeting with the Sphinx was the beginning of Oedipus' reputation and the victory by which Oedipus set himself apart from his contemporaries, including the prophet Tiresias, we can also see this incident as the most critical time of Oedipus' life, the moment of his greatest intellectual triumph, but also the moment in which his future downfall was determined. The Sphinx mytheme is thus, as a number of science fiction writers have recognized, one of the richest mythemes in all the Oedipus myth.

Some of the science fiction works in which the Sphinx mytheme plays an important part include H. G. Wells' *The Time Machine* (1895); Jules Verne's *An Antarctic Mystery* (*Le sphinx des glaces*, 1897); Philip José Farmer's "Riders of the Purple Wage: Or the Great Gavage" (1967) and *Venus on the Half-Shell* (1974); and Philip Dick and Roger Zelazny's *Deus Irae* (1976). Although published in the nineteenth century, Wells' and Verne's novels provide the first instances of the Sphinx' appearance in what would come to be called science fiction.[4] Significantly, these two men employ the Sphinx in totally opposite ways. Verne's picture is more positive, even simplistic, certainly naive, and has not inspired imitation. In contrast, Wells' portrayal of a diseased White Sphinx presiding over a degenerated society continues to evoke new associations and duplication. As the most resonant and influential Sphinx in science fiction, Wells' Sphinx deserves intensive study.

Wells' *The Time Machine*: The Sphinx as Subject and Subjectivity

The decaying, leprous Sphinx dominates the Time Traveller's adventures in the future. She is the first thing (besides hail and rhododendrons) that he sees when he arrives in the year 802,701, and she is mentioned or plays a part in almost one-third of his narrative. Indeed, so prevalent is this figure that the British edition of *The Time Machine* depicted the Sphinx on its cover, and numerous commentators have centered their studies on its role. Most of these interpretations take one of two tacks: the evolutionary/biological or the sociological/economical. A third approach—the psychological— has also been proposed and pursued but not yet privileged over the others, as I hope to show it should be. Once we see how the psychological predominates, we will also see how these other readings are transformed.

When first inspecting the object carved out of white stone, the Time Traveller concludes, "It was of white marble, in shape *something like* a winged sphinx, but the wings, instead of being carried vertically at the sides, were spread so that it seemed to hover."[5] The key words "something like" show that the Time Traveller has not absolutely identified the figure but has only descriptively approximated it. In fact, his entire description of this object vibrates with uncertainty, giving it the instability of a mirage. Not only does the figure *seem* to hover, but the pedestal *appears* to be of bronze, the sightless eyes *seem* to watch him, there is an unpleasant *suggestion* of disease, and the statue *seems* to advance and to recede as the hail gets thicker or thinner. Yet despite his initial hesitation, the Time

Traveller quickly turns ambiguity into certitude; for the rest of his trip, he refers to the figure as the "sphinx" or the "White Sphinx."

The significance of this identification cannot be stressed enough. For one thing, it indicates that in his first investigation of this alien land, the Time Traveller disregards his scientific training, which demands that personal impressions be supported with empirical evidence, and accepts a subjective reaction as fact. Why he does this is unclear, but what is clear is that the Time Traveller relates to the carved object—and the Sphinx he perceives in it—more from a psychological than a scientific standpoint. In consequence, all interpretations that we draw from the Sphinx' presence in this future world must be placed within the context of the Time Traveller's psychology. To state this another way, the Sphinx of 802,701 is not a ravaged icon; she is a mental projection of such an icon. The riddle Wells thus puts to the reader is, Why does the Time Traveller project a Sphinx into this world and why this particular Sphinx?

Numerous critics have surmised that the Sphinx' presence implies that the Time Traveller must solve a riddle, the most urgent one having to do with the nature of this strange humanity before him.[6] This assumption—inferred by relating the details of the Sphinx mytheme to the Time Traveller's situation—seems logical, although it must be revised to acknowledge that the Time Traveller has, by defining the prop, defined his role. Interestingly, the first function this prop serves for the Time Traveller is that of critic; she becomes the medium through which he chastises himself when he neglects his scientific training and presumes too much.

The Time Traveller admonishes himself by imagining the Sphinx smiling—at his astonishment over this new world or at his continuing ignorance of it. For example, after he spends a few hours with the Eloi, the Time Traveller believes that he has uncovered the secret to their world: he has "happened upon humanity upon the wane," and these delicate creatures are the evolutionary result of life made too easy for the human race (50). But no sooner does he advance this theory than he finds that his time machine has disappeared. In one quick turn of the back, mystery returns to this alien world; and the Sphinx, towering above the Time Traveller, seems to smile in mockery of his dismay (53). Such a smile reproves him for jumping to conclusions, and after foolishly trying to force entry into the pedestal, the Time Traveller finally takes the reproof to heart, realizing that "to sit among all those unknown things before a puzzle like that is hopeless. That way lies monomania. Face this world. Learn its ways, watch it, be careful of too hasty guesses at its meaning. In the end you will find clues to it all" (55).

One of the Time Traveller's reasons for turning the Sphinx into his conscience seems obvious. As a remnant from an age that prized intelligence and as a figure of wisdom herself,[7] the Sphinx holds powerful associations for reminding the Time Traveller to act accordingly in this future world. Connected to such associations, and equally relevant to *The Time Machine*, is Francis Bacon's designation of the Sphinx as a symbol of science:

> The fable [of the Sphinx] is an elegant and a wise one, invented apparently in allusion to Science: especially in its application to practical life . . . Sphinx proposes to men a variety of hard questions and riddles which she received from the Muses . . . when they pass from the Muses to Sphinx, that is from contemplation to practice . . . they begin to be painful and cruel: and unless they be solved and disposed of, they strangely torment and worry the mind, pulling it first this way and then that, and fairly tearing it to pieces.[8]

Bacon's account of the riddles that torture the scientist's mind closely resembles the Time Traveller's mental struggles with the mysteries of the world of 802,701. Finally, then, through the Sphinx, the Time Traveller reminds himself to be wise, to act above all like a scientist.

The correspondences between the Time Traveller's encounter with the White Sphinx and Oedipus' confrontation with the Theban Sphinx become even stronger once the Time Traveller discovers that his time machine is hidden within the Sphinx' pedestal. Now the answer to the Sphinx' riddle—what is the nature of this world?— can literally be found inside the Sphinx in the form of the Morlocks, whose existence the Time Traveller has yet to fully apprehend. Moreover, to venture inside the White Sphinx is to risk being devoured, just as Oedipus did when he faced the Sphinx who ravaged Thebes. The White Sphinx has turned sinister; and from this point on in the story, she becomes more of a monster than a guide.

The White Sphinx' role as devouring monster does not stop, or even start, at the phenomenal level. To move inside this creature, which we have already identified as a projection of the Time Traveller's psyche, is to move to the place of the unconscious. Behind the doors of the Sphinx' pedestal lies a dark, underground network of tunnels and caves, the subterranean home of the cannibalistic Morlocks. Such details in themselves lead one to associate this world with the nightmare scene of the unconscious. Further support comes from psychoanalytic interpretations that see the Sphinx as the Terrible Mother. This association has been made most prominently by Erich Neumann who sees the Sphinx-Terrible Mother as "the all-inclusive symbol of [the] devouring aspect of the unconscious."[9] Within this perspective, "all dangerous affects and impulses, all the evils which come up from the unconscious and overwhelm the ego with their dynamism" are the Terrible Mother's progeny (161). The hero who conquers the Sphinx thus breaks away from the despotic rule of the unconscious. His victory brings with it "a new spiritual status, a new knowledge, and an alteration of consciousness" (161).

Psychologically, then, the Time Traveller's confrontation with the White Sphinx includes the challenge of leaving the daylight garden of his consciousness (the world of the Eloi) and entering the nightmare underground of his unconscious (the world of the Morlocks). Not only are the Morlocks mysterious enemies that the Time Traveller must come to know in order to survive and escape this future time, they are also mental demons (the Sphinx' "progeny") that he must face and deal with. Such a reading helps to explain the Time Traveller's intense dread of these creatures—a dread that either paralyzes him or excites him to violence.[10] For example, having decided that he will have to "descend for the solution of my difficulties" (61), the Time Traveller cannot act for two days: "I felt assured that the Time Machine was only to be recovered by boldly penetrating these underground mysteries. Yet I could not face the mystery . . . even to clamber down into the darkness of the well appalled me" (64).

Once he does explore this cavernous world and barely escapes with his life, the Time Traveller grows increasingly desirous of murdering "a Morlock or so." "Very inhuman," he suggests to his listeners, "to want to go killing one's own descendants! But it was impossible, somehow, to feel any humanity in the things" (74).

David Lake proposes that the Time Traveller's excessive response to the Morlocks derives from his repressed fear of personal and racial death.[11] Other critics, following Bernard Bergonzi's lead, have argued that the Time Traveller reveals here a "contemporary bourgeois fear of the working class," which the Morlocks stand for on one level.[12] While plausible, such theories do not seem to provide the whole story. According to Lake, the Time Traveller does not regard the Morlocks as human, because "he has subconsciously equated them with the great and last Enemy [death]."[13] To the contrary, as we will see, the Time Traveller's unconscious identification with these descendants explains his irrational dread; rather than being inhuman, they are all too human.

Significantly, although the similarities between the Time Traveller and the Morlocks seem numerous and blatant (much more so than those between himself and the Eloi), the Time Traveller remains blind to them. For one, like the Morlocks, the Time Traveller resorts to force when cunning will not work. He violently shakes the Eloi when they do not act as he thinks they should (53, 55), and he even seems to relish his hand-to-hand combat with the Morlocks, feeling "the succulent giving of flesh and bone" when he hits them (79) and being "almost sorry" when he does not have to use his iron bar against them during his seige of the White Sphinx (82). The Time Traveller also shares the Morlocks' carnivorous appetite. Upon returning to his own time, he is "starving for a bit of meat" (39) and declares, "What a treat it is to stick a fork into meat again!" (40). The meat he drools after may not be human, but still the Time Traveller misses the fact that his "carnal cravings" (47) link him as closely to the Morlocks as his fruit eating does to the frugivorous Eloi. Finally, like the Morlocks, he, too, works with machines, spending most of the daylight hours locked away in his laboratory fiddling with mechanical devices. Indeed, the few details we are given about his workshop make it sound very similar to the Morlocks' network of tunnels, caverns, and entry wells: a long, draughty corridor connects the lab to the main part of the house (37); a door leads from it to the garden (90); and much of the room's light seems to be channeled through a skylight, which is broken by the wind created when the Time Traveller operates the time machine a second time (89).[14]

The Time Traveller justifies his attacks against the Morlocks by picturing them as beasts rather than as humans, but such a defense also enables him to ignore just how much he shares with them. To meet them is to meet a part of himself, the part that is often thought of as base or primitive—the cannibalistic warrior who uses his physical strength and cunning to rule weaker members of his race.[15] And although the Time Traveller finally gathers the courage to descend into the Morlocks' lair and to struggle with them, in the end he seems unable to admit to his consciousness the full meaning of these encounters. He retreats wildly from this underground world and scrambles crazily within the pedestal of the Sphinx to escape the Morlocks' presence completely. His returns to the upper world of the Eloi or to his home in Victorian England are, in other words, retreats to the safety of repression.

But just because the Time Traveller cannot face the darkness of himself does not mean that he fails to contrive an answer to the Sphinx' riddle. In fact, he recognizes that the Morlocks have descended from the human race, despite being unable to relate that devolution to himself personally. The way he gets around such personalizing of the future is to find its roots in the labor practices of nineteenth-century England. His final theory about the world of 802,701—his answer to the Sphinx' riddle—is that the physical separation of capitalists and laborers in his own world led to a biological split within the human race in the future: "So, as I see it, the Upperworld man had drifted towards his feeble prettiness, and the Underworld to mere mechanical industry" (82).

This combined biological and sociological explanation for the situation the Time Traveller finds in the future moves us, finally, to similar critical interpretations of the White Sphinx. Within such views, the Sphinx stands both as a sign of the regression of the human race and as an ironic reminder of a superior state of civilization. For example, David Lake suggests that the White Sphinx' decaying condition recalls the final part of the Theban Sphinx' riddle—man in his old age—so that we recognize in her appearance "the decay of Man in the future world" and "the menace of imminent death."[16] John Huntington points to the paradox in this symbolization: "The future is represented by a monument that we associate with early civilization." Existing among a people who can no longer value or even comprehend her history, the Sphinx "is a figure of the very intellectual prowess that the childish creatures of the future lack."[17]

As the Time Traveller's final theory about the future indicates, the evolutionary/biological level of interpretation is so closely joined in *The Time Machine* (and indeed throughout Wells' works) to the sociological/economic that they can hardly be separated. According to Roslynn Haynes, "The Darwinian emphasis on the continual struggle for survival had made Wells keenly aware of the parallel existential struggle in sociology and politics."[18] In fact, Huntington suggests that Wells may have drawn his view of the Sphinx from a passage in Thomas H. Huxley's "The Struggle for Existence in Human Society" (1888), in which Huxley argues that competition will continue to divide the human race into the miserable poor and the monstrously wealthy. "It [this uneven state of affairs] is the true riddle of the Sphinx; and every nation which does not solve it will sooner or later be devoured by the monster itself has generated."[19]

Whether Huxley's interpretation of the Sphinx directly influenced Wells or not, it certainly parallels the sociological explanations given by the Time Traveller in his several attempts to ascertain the relationship between the Eloi and the Morlocks. But in the end all theories, both ours and the Time Traveller's, about the White Sphinx and the future come back to the Time Traveller's psychology. Catherine Rainwater states that the Sphinx forces the Time Traveller "to discover the extent to which the human mind projects meanings onto the exterior world."[20] More accurately, the Time Traveller, through the medium of a Sphinx that he mentally creates and animates, gradually comes to appreciate the difficulty, perhaps the impossibility, of escaping one's own subjectivity. As he concludes after positing his final sociological/evolutionary explanation for the state of affairs in the world of 802,701: "It may be as wrong an explanation as mortal wit could invent. It is how the thing shaped itself to me, and as that I give it to you" (82).

The Time Traveller's answer to the riddle of the White Sphinx might be more tentative than Oedipus' instant reply "man"—even though several critics have suggested that, when reduced to its simplest formulation, the Time Traveller's answer is the same as Oedipus'—but the outcomes of their encounters are, in fact, very similar. The conjunction lies in the paradoxes that attend each man's meeting with the Sphinx. One of the most important paradoxes in Oedipus' confrontation has to do with his status as savior. In the opening scene of *Oedipus the King*, the priest tells Oedipus:

> It was you, we remember, a newcomer to Cadmus' town,
> That broke our bondage to the vile Enchantress.
> With no foreknowledge or hint that we could give,
> But, as we truly believe, with the help of God,
> You gave us back our life. [21]

The priest's encomium reminds us that Oedipus' victory over the Sphinx held societal as well as personal implications. As Alister Cameron notes, "For his conquest of the Sphinx, Oedipus is accounted a 'savior.'. . . This puts him in a class, we could say, with those other heroes like Heracles and Theseus, who made the world safe for men by ridding it of the monsters; although Oedipus' victory is perhaps even more distinguished in being a triumph of the human intelligence over the forces of darkness" (21).

But the delivery of Thebes and the victory of Oedipus are provisional and double edged. By granting Oedipus sovereignty over their city, the Thebans unwittingly give asylum to both a patricide and a regicide as well as enable incest. In accepting his new position, Oedipus finishes fulfilling the fate prescribed for him by the oracle: he marries his mother. Oedipus' exchange with the Sphinx marks, then, the transition from one state of existence to another—for Thebes, from afflicted wasteland to thriving city; for Oedipus, from wanderer to king, from ordinary man to extraordinary man. However, the most important change for both parties is yet to come: that which takes them from blind innocence to blinding irony. Thebes is revitalized only to be stricken with another plague; Oedipus is elevated by means of his intelligence only to be crushed by his ignorance.[22] Cameron succinctly explains Sophocles' dramatic strategy in regard to the Sphinx: "Once we are past the prologue, it becomes apparent that Sophocles is not celebrating Oedipus' victory; rather, he has set it up prominently to bring out a great irony he sees in it" (21). Indeed, as Cameron concludes, "All appearances to the contrary, Oedipus failed the test of the Sphinx; . . . the celebrated *sophia* amounts to nothing when Oedipus does not know himself" (22).

Like Oedipus' triumph, the Time Traveller's escape from the White Sphinx poses numerous complications. When he tries to pass on his knowledge about the future to various representative men of his own time, he is met with skepticism, incredulity, and the diagnosis that he suffers from overwork. Of the Time Traveller's guests, only Hillyer takes the story to heart and believes it enough to transmit it to us. However, as with many time travel narratives, *The Time Machine* does not answer the hanging question of whether we *can* change events of the past or future—or, equally important, whether the changes we make will, ironically, bring about the very future we are trying to evade. In brief, when Wells' novel ends, the Time Traveller is poised between triumph and tragedy, between Oedipus' community-saving encounter with the Sphinx and his later discovery that he has brought misery to his land. Lacking a modern counterpart to *Oedipus at Colonus*, we are left to write our own sequel in the way we choose to live.

Verne's *An Antarctic Mystery*: The Sphinx and the Riddles of Science

In *An Antarctic Mystery*, Jules Verne also employs the Sphinx mytheme, and like Wells, he presents the Sphinx as a sort of avatar of science. Although this is where the similarities between their Sphinxes end, it is enough to remind us that both men grew up in an age when many people of the Western world believed that science would eventually solve the mysteries of the universe. However, Verne's straightforward presentation contrasts vividly with the complex rendering of the Sphinx mytheme that I inferred in *The Time Machine*. A brief look at Verne's novel will reveal why its Sphinx has become a literary dinosaur, whereas Wells' White Sphinx continues to spawn meaning and imitators.

Verne composed *An Antarctic Mystery* as a sequel to Edgar Allan Poe's "The Narrative of A. Gordon Pym," picking up Poe's characters eleven years after we last left them drifting toward a gigantic white figure in the Antarctic Ocean.[23] Verne's plot centers upon Captain Len Guy's search for his brother William, captain of *The Jane* in Poe's story. The search retraces the path of Pym, who accompanied William Guy. Indeed, two members of the crew, Joerling (the narrator) and Hunt (who finally reveals himself to be Dirk Peters, Pym's half-breed companion in Poe's story), are mainly interested in finding Pym since Peters believes that Pym never returned to America and, therefore, could never have met Poe, who presents Pym's story to the public. After numerous adventures and tribulations, both William Guy and Pym are located. Guy is emaciated but alive; Pym has not been so fortunate. He has died near the Antarctic Pole, pinned by his musket—secured in his belt—to a colossal magnet shaped like a Sphinx.

The Antarctic Sphinx is both a natural wonder and a symbol. On the material level, she is lodestone whose prodigious power of attraction can be scientifically explained as Joerling tells us: "The Tradewinds bring a constant succession of clouds or mists in which immense quantities of electricity not completely exhausted by storms, are stored. Hence there exists a formidable accumulation of electric fluid at the poles, and it flows towards the land in a permanent stream." A block of iron subjected to these currents would turn into a magnet with power "proportioned to the intensity of the current, to the number of turns of the electric helix, and to the square root of the diameter of the block of magnetized iron."[24] This gigantic lodestone has apparently only coincidentally assumed the shape of "the winged monster which Grecian mythology has placed upon the way to Thebes" (317).

But Joerling also attaches figurative meaning to this natural marvel. For him, the Antarctic Sphinx holds those truths of nature that humans have yet to grasp. Discoveries of great value remain to be made in these waters, he contends, and so other explorers must follow Pym and "wrest the last Antarctic Mystery from the Sphinx of the Ice-realm" (335–36). As Joerling sees it, only time stands in the way of this Oedipal victory over the Sphinx, that is, of the scientist's mastery of nature.[25]

Neither Joerling nor Verne attaches any irony to Oedipus' meeting with the Sphinx or to science's future, but nothing dates *An Antarctic Mystery* more than Joerling's confidence that we will someday know all of nature's secrets. In fact, such confidence was already waning by the time Verne's novel was translated into English and Wells' *The Time Machine* was published. One source reflecting the changing opinion was F. S. C. Schiller's appropriately titled *Riddles of the Sphinx: A Study in the Philosophy of Evolution* (first edition 1891). In this work Schiller tried to counter the growing pessimism caused by not being able to know the meaning of life, by not having a comprehensive and ultimate metaphysical system. Schiller's defense of positivism—we should seek to know because we must and ought—still forms a current of thought in certain philosophic and scientific schools, but its correlative—that we *will* know—has lost a great deal of viability. Werner Heisenberg's uncertainty principle (1927) and Kurt Gödel's theorem (1931) are just two of many ground-breaking theories that reject the notion of absolute and final knowledge, the former in regard to subatomic particles, the latter in connection with mathematical systems. Because twentieth-century epistemology has moved more and more toward admitting a measure of indeterminacy, Verne's Sphinx has become trapped in the nineteenth-century—restrained by the specific and now passe—interpretation that Verne's narrator gives it.

In this comparison of Verne's novel to Wells', I do not want to leave readers with the impression that the best work is the one whose mytheme (or mythemes) leads (lead) us in the most directions. Quantity does not qualify as quality. However, I do want to make clear that, while the mytheme holds great power to inspire authors and readers, not every appearance of a mytheme inspires the same level of reader involvement. Such an implication would come dangerously close to reviving the once popular—and, I think, fallacious—argument that incorporating myth into a narrative automatically increases that narrative's resonance and meaning, turning bad fiction into good and making good fiction better. Fiction is not a base metal that can be transformed into gold by the touch of myth. What makes Verne's use of the Sphinx mytheme less successful than Wells' is not the limited number of interpretations that it inspires but the limited validity of the interpretation that Verne gives it. Wells' more ambiguous and psychological use of the Sphinx mytheme has, I think, allowed readers to continue to ascribe new meaning to his White Sphinx and has thus kept that Sphinx alive.

Farmer, Dick, and Zelazny: The Anti-Sphinx Meets the Anti-Oedipus

Three recent science fiction stories that have employed the Sphinx mytheme include Philip José Farmer's novel *Venus on the Half-Shell*, his short story "Riders of the Purple Wage: Or the Great Gavage," and Philip Dick and Roger Zelazny's collaborative novel *Deus Irae*. Although none of these works capitalizes on the Sphinx mytheme to the extent that *The Time Machine* does—avoiding especially the psychological angle—they all use this mytheme to darken their pessimistic visions of the future. In this darkening, these narratives recall Wells' rendering of the Sphinx mytheme. In other words, our understanding of Wells' use of the Sphinx mytheme informs our understanding of these writers' use of the same mytheme. The intertextuality that the mytheme evokes can thus extend from narrative to narrative as well as from narrative to myth.

In both his stories, Farmer combines the Egyptian Sphinx of Giza and the Theban Sphinx to emphasize that the moral and intellectual disintegration of the human race has crossed continents. *Venus* begins with the protagonist, Simon Wagstaff, making love to his fiancée on the head of the Sphinx of Giza while tourists sightsee below. Although this Egyptian Sphinx has a different history and geography than the Sphinx of Thebes, Simon makes clear that they are figuratively akin. In Simon's world, a futuristic version of our own, the Sphinx has become a landmark, a spectacle to be photographed and played upon. During his recital of the Sphinx' history, Simon underscores the fact that his contemporaries not only fail to appreciate what the Sphinx once represented but are incapable of doing so. As a consequence of this universal deterioration, Simon, who has taken over the Sphinx' habit of asking difficult questions, observes that he need not fear having to commit suicide, as did the Theban Sphinx, since no one seems able to answer him. Indeed, in comparing the two guidebooks on the Sphinx of Giza, he discovers that experts of his era cannot even correctly measure the Sphinx' dimensions.

Simon's evaluation of the Earth's sorry state gains almost instant substantiation when a flood kills every living being—except for Simon, a dog, and an owl. As Simon later learns, this deluge is produced by the Hoonors, a race that has assumed the task of cleaning up the universe by destroying any society, like Simon's, that pollutes its planet. Here Farmer mixes the familiar myth of Noah—or the less well-known myth of Deucalion or the flood narrative in the Babylonian *Gilgamesh*[26]—with the Sphinx mytheme to insinuate that the lack of wisdom is a mortal sin. And even though the Hoonors' descendants, whom Simon meets thousands of years later, are slightly ashamed of their ancestors' radical response to the Earth's condition, they submit that "Earth is now a nice clean planet, which it wouldn't be if we hadn't done what we did."[27]

Farmer's use of the Sphinx in his earlier story "Riders of the Purple Wage" closely parallels that in *Venus*. Set primarily in Los Angeles in 2166, "Riders" reveals the dystopian consequences of believing that a leisure society will lead to utopia. The United States government has recently decided to provide its citizens with all material needs so they can devote themselves to developing their artistic tendencies. However, in devising this plan, the government leaders

failed to consider that "only about ten per cent of the population—
if that—are inherently capable of producing anything worth while,
or even mildly interesting, in the arts."[28] Most people spend their
time drinking, watching "fido" (a technologically superior form of
television), fornicating, eating, and playing cards. In addition, the
new policy has not altered one bit the place of the artist, represented
by Chibiabos Elgreco Winnegan. Chib is misunderstood, unappreci-
ated, fawned over by sycophants, and drained of time and energy
by parasites, including his mother. The government's attempt to
achieve utopia has produced exactly the opposite effect. Ironically,
Chib's world desperately needs the one individual the government
thought it was building a nation of: the artist, someone who can stir
citizens out of their lethargy and inspire them to action.

Chib's grandfather, Win-again Winnegan, is the only person wise
enough to understand this need and also to see Chib's potential to
satisfy it. Nearly twenty-five years earlier, Win-again pulled the
Crime of the Age by stealing twenty billion dollars from the federal
deposit vault; he then faked his own death and has since been hiding
out in a secret room in Chib and his mother's house. Only Chib
knows for certain that his grandfather lives, although government
agents suspect the ruse and are investigating. To Chib, this cranky
120-year-old man has a face like "the wind-beaten, sandblown Sphinx
of Gizeh" (46); and to be sure, the homespun writing of "Grandpa,"
his unpublished "How I Screwed Uncle Sam & Other Private Ejacu-
lations," rings with sarcastic truth.

But Grandpa Winnegan is not the only Sphinx in Farmer's story.
He himself tells Chib that the New Sphinx, born of the old one
whose riddle Oedipus solved, is "a smartass kid with a question
nobody's been able to answer yet"; namely, "What, then, is Man?"
(46). To Grandpa Winnegan, Chib is a Hercules, a stumblebum
Apollo, an "Edipus Wrecked" (59); but he is in danger of succumbing
to the vices of his society by "painting with his penis and not with
his heart." In a note written before his death but delivered after it,
the old man advises his grandson to "go to Egypt. Steep yourself in
the ancient culture. Stand before the Sphinx. Ask her (actually, it's
a he) the Question" (101). Farmer thus suggests that artists must

appropriate the New Sphinx' question and turn it back upon her/ him since, in posing it, she/he must also know its answer. If Chib is to become a true artist, he must do what all great artists have done: break free of all support systems (his mother as well as his government), seek the dark mysteries of human nature, and transmit his vision through his art. Chib's archetypal journey would be rare in any age, but in Farmer's version of the twenty-second century, where conflict and even travel have been reduced to a minimum, such a journey is novel. This also makes it urgent.

The devolution of the world can become even more obvious when the Sphinx is made active, as she is in Dick and Zelazny's *Deus Irae*. Here, the Sphinx' role is adopted by the Great C, a computer created by Carl Lufteufel, who has been named the "God of Wrath," because he invented and activated the "great objectless device" that propelled the world into an atomic war and its subsequent nuclear winter. Damaged in the war, the Great C has degenerated from a venerated source of knowledge—although even in its prime, Lufteufel made it do "insane" things[29]—to an infamous bogey. It occupies a vast chamber, full of bats and spiders, in a dilapidated house and is in danger of losing its memory and power. To replenish its data base, the Great C must feed upon the psychic energy of humans, which it does by sending out a peripatetic extension of itself (most frequently in female form) to kill any passerby who fails to ask it an unanswerable question.

But while this nasty practice has earned the Great C a widespread reputation, a difficult feat in a world whose population and communication channels have been drastically cut, the computer's broken-down condition ensures that each interview will be more comic, or pathetic, than tragic. Structurally deficient, the Great C has lost confidence in its answers, indulges in sentimental reminiscences of its former greatness, and when its artificial intelligence fails, violates the rules of the game by resorting to violence. Its confrontations are travesties of the legendary meeting between Oedipus and the Sphinx. They merely emphasize the intellectual and heroic distance separating this postatomic world from that ancient one.

I have said a great deal about the Sphinx in these last three stories and not so much about Oedipus, yet an impotent or silent Sphinx is not enough in itself to assure a dystopian vision of the future. In fact, the destruction of incompetence would be a cleansing of sorts—as Farmer's *Venus* suggests—and a world where at least one person associates a silent Sphinx with the loss of wisdom would not be totally vacuous, since it takes wisdom to recognize this loss. It is therefore significant that each of these three science fiction stories, like *The Time Machine*, shades in its pessimistic picture by compromising either the Oedipus figure or the Oedipus role.

For instance, in *Venus* the redemptive role played by Oedipus is entirely circumvented when the human race and the Sphinx are destroyed by an outside force. If this story presents us with an Oedipus figure, it would have to be Simon Wagstaff. And, indeed, his encounter with (upon?) the Sphinx of Giza could be seen as a turning point in his life and in the life of the Earth. However, this meeting actually marks a change in milieu, not in mien. After the Sphinx and all human beings are destroyed, Simon merely focuses his search for answers upon a single question—Why are we born only to suffer and die?—while he expands the target of his interrogation to the cosmos. He is more Job or Odysseus than Oedipus.

In *Deus Irae*, Tibor McMasters—a talented painter who is an "incomplete," that is, a mutant born without arms and legs—asks the Great C an unanswerable question (How did the universe begin?), and he escapes her clutches by shooting her full of bullets. This violent confrontation in which rules are made to be broken seems a far cry from Oedipus and the Sphinx' battle of wits. Certainly, Tibor's defeat of the Great C does little by itself to revive his postatomic world. Of course, if he *had* been captured by this Sphinx-like computer, he never would have, unknowingly, killed Carl Lufteufel, the God of Wrath—an act that lifts the evil atmosphere enveloping Earth since the war. If Tibor fulfills Oedipus' role of saving the land, he does not do it through conquering the Sphinx but simply because he survived the meeting.

Finally, "Riders of the Purple Wage" does not contain a definite Oedipus figure, but it does offer a prospective Oedipus. Should Chib accept Grandpa Winnegan's advice to confront the New Sphinx and ask him/her the vital question, we can assume that he will then be more psychologically fit to create the kind of art that might save his land. However, such a rendezvous is not inevitable; nor can we suppose that if it does take place, it will precipitate the necessary renewal. As with *The Time Machine*, we can only guess at what the future holds. Still, the apparent promise of this meeting slightly lessens the pessimism of Farmer's futuristic vision and thus supplies a ray of light that cuts through the shadow cast by the Sphinx in science fiction.

Answering the Riddle of the Anti-Sphinx

This chapter has shown that, except for Wells, most science fiction writers who have incorporated the Sphinx mytheme into their stories have been more interested in the positive side of Oedipus' encounter with the Sphinx than in its less pleasant features (specifically, its contiguous destruction or its part in moving Oedipus and Thebes toward greater tragedy). All these writers, including Wells, have assumed that readers will remember Oedipus as the heroic savior who matched wits with a worthy opponent and, in winning the contest, cured an afflicted land. Yet, ironically, they reveal this assumption by presenting readers with the negative to this positive picture. In employing and altering this mytheme, these writers usually ask readers to measure the present or a future world against that ancient one, frozen in a moment of heroic battle.

The first difference between the classical world and the future one may be found in the character of the Sphinx herself. With the exception of Verne's *An Antarctic Mystery*, every science fiction story in which this mytheme appears is dystopian, with the Sphinx either acting within or presiding over a wasteland.[30] Importantly, though, the science fiction Sphinx is usually not the cause of the destruction that surrounds her; in fact, she is typically as much a victim as are the human beings who confront her. Whether silently passive or ineptly active, these Sphinxes consequently stand as ironic reminders of heroism and intelligence in worlds that have essentially forgotten how to be either brave or wise.

In "Revivals of Ancient Mythologies in Current Science Fiction and Fantasy," Casey Fredericks observes that a "mutant, post-atomic world [can plunge] the remnant of mankind into a time when heroism of the ancient Greek type is both possible and necessary."[31] By expanding this observation to include any world where "being alive" consists primarily of satisfying appetites and instincts, we reach a fairly accurate assessment of the worlds found in the dystopian stories studied in this chapter. But our analysis of these narratives suggests that ripeness for heroism is not all and that, in fact, myths can be used to increase the dystopian dimensions of a world rather than to reveal the capacity of humans for greatness. One might justifiably wonder whether these stories refuse redemption because they realize that it always carries a price, especially if someone like Oedipus is the deliverer. However, only *The Time Machine* shows any sign that it might be playing one irony off another. And even so, its final message seems to be the same as that of the later stories: we and our descendants cannot count on the immediate salvation allowed in myth.

C H A P T E R   4

Mythemes and Questions of Genre: The Blindness of the Private Eye in Antidetective Fiction

■

Tzvetan Todorov observes that any study of genre must begin by describing structure,[1] and since implicit mythemes are structural units of the text, it seems inevitable that our pursuit of such signs will eventually lead to the level of genre. In other words, the dialogue that the mytheme asks us to initiate between myth and fiction need not stop with issues related to a particular story; often—especially when we begin to explore several similar stories—this dialogue will be pushing beyond the area of the text into that of genre. Such is the case with the Oedipus myth's appearance in the antidetective story, a postmodern offspring of the detective story. In reading such stories, we discover that our search for the meaning of various implicit mythemes forces us to rethink issues of genre classification. To put this another way, if chapter 3 revealed how deep into a story a single mytheme can take us, the investigation here will show how very far outside a story we can go and still remain within its purview. It will also provide additional proof that the exchange between myth and modern fiction is an equal one, with fiction speaking as much to the myth (casting new light on it) as the myth does to fiction.

The Oedipus myth's appearance in the detective story seems even less surprising than its presence in science fiction. After all, one of the more persistent, if minor, literary controversies of the twentieth century has centered on whether Sophocles' *Oedipus the King* is a detective story, perhaps even the first. Although we simplify to reduce this debate to two sides, in general the lines of argument have been rather predictable, with popular culture critics affirming the attribution and classical scholars denying it.[2] Given the vested interests of each side, this debate seemed headed toward a permanent deadlock and, more importantly, a moot court attended only by the parties involved. However, the surfacing of the Oedipus myth *not* in the detective story per se but in its postmodern offshoot, the antidetective story, has revitalized this debate and increased its significance.

According to Stefano Tani, who has studied this strain of postmodern fiction at length, antidetective writers use detective conventions "with the precise intention of expressing the disorder and the existential void they find central to our time in a genre [the detective story] designed to epitomize the contrary." Consequently, they "dismantle the elegant engine Poe constructed, pulling apart the once functional machinery and removing its pieces (now the plot, now the suspense technique, now the clichéd detective) to do different things with them."[3] If Sophocles' play were a conventional whodunit, then we would expect it to be part of the "machinery" dismantled by antidetective fiction, that its plot would serve primarily as a target of parody. What we find, however, is nearly the opposite.

In three significant antidetective novels—Alain Robbe-Grillet's *The Erasers* (1953), Michel Butor's *Passing Time* (1957), and Thomas Pynchon's *The Crying of Lot 49* (1966)—the Oedipus myth actually helps to overturn detective fiction conventions. This subversive role suggests that if *Oedipus the King* deserves entry into any genre other than tragedy, it should be as a precursor of antidetective fiction rather than as the first detective story. Equally important, although each narrative uses the Oedipus myth in a slightly different way, they all use it to the end of turning the reader into a detective. Because the Oedipus myth thus serves double duty in these novels, they are more difficult to read and analyze than the science fiction works examined in chapter 3. The mystery novel becomes not only a story about a mystery but also a mystery itself; and the reader is like the detective, who is like Oedipus, who is like the reader. In sum, *Oedipus the King* mediates between detective fiction and postmodernist antidetective fiction, and Oedipus himself links the experiences of the readers of both.

The structure of the detective story varies, but in its standard, skeletal form, it is plotted around a murder and the investigating detective. George Burton, the mystery writer in Butor's *Passing Time*, adds flesh to this basic anatomy: the criminal commits the first murder, the detective the second, killing the criminal with "the explosion of truth" (143–44). In addition, Burton notes, these acts occupy a special place in the mystery novel. The story begins with the crime, "the climax of all the dramatic events which the detective has to rediscover gradually" (167), and ends when the detective is able to reconstruct that crime step-by-deliberate-step. In other words, unlike the spy novel or the thriller, the whodunit is a relatively bloodless affair. Most of its gruesome violence takes place offstage and is reported in retrospect. As Todorov puts it, the detective novel contains "the story of the crime and the story of the investigation"; the first story must end before the second begins, and in the second, the characters do not act, but learn.[4]

The antidetective narrative subverts this structure and alters its inner significance. One way to accomplish this subversion is by reversing the order of the two stories so that the investigation precedes the crime, making the detective appear inept and dense, as in *The Erasers*. Another line of attack is to collapse the two stories so that the sleuth learns finally that he or she is the culprit, as happens in all the novels examined in this chapter. This collapse actually constitutes an important breakdown of the classical detective story in that it assaults one of the genre's most respected imperatives: the detective must never be the criminal.[5] So strongly have detective story devotees felt about this separation that it is often listed among rules for detective writers,[6] and an author who comes close to violating it spurs controversy—as did Agatha Christie in *The Murder of Roger Ackroyd*, in which the narrator, *not* the detective, is revealed to be the murderer.[7]

The Erasers, Passing Time, and *The Crying of Lot 49* all attack this powerful convention through inverting the detective story structure. Wallas, Jacques Revel, and Oedipa Maas are detectives—the first a professional, the other two amateurs—whose investigations lead to self-incrimination. But the appearance of the Oedipus myth in these novels reminds us that Sophocles collapsed the detective-criminal dichotomy almost 2,500 years ago, *ante facto*, we might say. In fact, it is difficult to tell whether Robbe-Grillet, Butor, and Pynchon resolved their stories with this circularity because they were attempting to subvert the detective form or because they decided to use the Oedipus myth. But as we will see, this question of motives is irrelevant. An author could hardly contemplate the collapse of the detective-criminal duality without invoking Oedipus, nor could one think of Oedipus without expecting such a collapse.

Sophocles' tragedy initially looks like a detective story, as does the antidetective story, in that its principal action begins with attending to a murder (albeit a rather tardy attending) and is spent upon investigating that crime. It becomes an antidetective story however when the pursuer turns out to be the pursued. Or, to straighten out the chronology here, Sophocles' drama offers the narrative structure for one type of antidetective story, a type built upon three mythemes: the disclosure of a death (12); the investigation surrounding that death (13); and the investigator's recognition of his or her complicity (15). The first two mythemes form the structural core of the detective tale, but when the third is deployed, we have moved into the realm of the antidetective.

But if the structure of *Oedipus the King* seems to constitute one kind of antidetective story, the final significance of its denouement does not. Critics studying this postmodern form observe that its sine qua non is the refusal to conclude with the neat, absolute solution that is the whodunit's trademark. William Spanos associates this refusal with the reaction against "the rigidly causal plot of the well-made work of the humanistic tradition, as catering to and thus further hardening the expectation of the rational solution generated by the scientific analysis of the man-in-the-world."[8] Most antidetective novels end without explaining the mystery, indeed, often seem not to end at all but simply to stop. In *The Erasers, Passing Time,* and *The Crying of Lot 49* the detective's self-incrimination supports that open ending by giving a circularity to the plot that suggests not the tying up of loose ends but the endless repetition of mysteries.

As Aristotle adduced by choosing it as the model of the well-constructed tragic plot, *Oedipus the King* does not seem to conclude indeterminately. Oedipus' self-blinding and exile declare that the case, satisfactorily resolved, is closed and justice administered. If Sophocles' drama is to be grouped then with the likes of *The Erasers* and *The Crying of Lot 49*, we will have to address the problem of how a play within the Aristotelian tradition of the causal plot can also be part of a movement attacking that tradition. In order to answer that question, let us first look closely at the antidetective form by examining such novels using the Oedipus myth. With a firmer grasp of the materials and motives of this form, we will be in a better position to determine how the Oedipus myth relates to this postmodern genre—or, more accurately, how this postmodern genre relates to the Oedipus myth.

Robbe-Grillet's *The Erasers*: Readers in Search of Oedipus

In the most comprehensive exploration of the Oedipus myth in *The Erasers*, Bruce Morrissette maintains that the myth is the key to comprehending the novel, its basic structuring principle.[9] Morrissette breaks down this structuring function into three roles: intellectual parody, mythic parallel, and psychiatric unifying principle (66). As we will see, Morrissette's analysis of these roles not only misses several ways that Robbe-Grillet uses the Oedipus myth to entice readers into interacting with his text, but it also misstates the psychoanalytic principle rendered through the myth. Nevertheless, Morrissette's identifications provide an essential starting point for exploring this complex novel.

To realize the first two roles that Morrissette assigns to the Oedipus myth, we need only briefly review the novel's plot. On the evening of October 26, Daniel Dupont, a semiretired economics professor living in an unidentified town (presumably in Flanders), is reported dead from a gunshot wound to the chest inflicted at 7:30

p.m. Because of certain details, the authorities link Dupont's death to a group of anarchists that has been murdering a victim daily for the last eight days. The Bureau of Investigation sends a special agent, Wallas, who spends the day of October 27 questioning witnesses and visiting the scene of the crime, to which he returns that evening. At precisely 7:30 p.m., he shoots and kills an intruder whom he assumes to be the murderer. Later he discovers that the victim is Dupont himself.

As Morrissette points out, this sequence of events approximates that of *Oedipus the King* while simultaneously subverting it. Like Oedipus, Wallas fulfills the detective's role of solving a murder when he discovers that he himself is the murderer he seeks; but, unlike Oedipus, Wallas commits the crime after he begins his investigation. Indeed, he becomes the murderer only by being the detective. As Jean Ricardou puts it, "The enquiry *precedes* the murder and, in preceding it, *engenders* it."[10]

But Morrissette neglects to point out that we are not able to confirm the resemblance between the plot of *The Erasers* and that of *Oedipus the King* until we reach the end of the book. To put this another way, Robbe-Grillet never lets our hindsight become foresight. From the moment we read the novel's epigraph taken from *Oedipus the King*, we are cast into the role of a detective who suspects that the Oedipus myth might hold the key to the novel. The early appearance of other references—such as the Sphinx-like creature that Garanati imagines he sees in the river and the curtains printed with the foundling motif scattered throughout the town[11]—encourages that suspicion. As Morrissette's "incomplete" twelve-page review of these references reveals, the town is literally littered with the Oedipus myth. The most compelling such sign is the unknown brand of eraser for which Wallas hunts—containing the middle syllable *di*, a first syllable of at least two letters, and a last syllable of two or three letters—which possibly works out to *Oedipos* or *Oedipe*.

However, rather than confirming the Oedipus myth's importance, this littering has the opposite effect. One or two signals to the myth's presence are all we really need. More than that seems superfluous, a barrage that either insults our powers of critical perception or, at best, throws the status of the myth into doubt. Moreover, as detailed in chapter 2, to identify any explicit mytheme as a structural element we must be able to show that its essential action occurs implicitly in the narrative. We can fulfill this requirement for the Oedipal mythemes in *The Erasers* only by pushing our case. Before Wallas shoots Dupont, two such mythemes—the discovery of a death and the investigation into that death—do materialize, yet these actions are too common to the detective novel to designate them solely as Oedipal. In short, instead of becoming more secure about the myth's place, we grow uncertain (will the plot follow the myth or not?), possibly confused (what is Robbe-Grillet up to?), or, in some cases, skeptical about the seriousness of this mythic parallel.

The Oedipal content of *The Erasers* thus vacillates between meaninglessness and meaningfulness. Until the story's climax, readers have no real cause to see the references to the Oedipus myth as anything more than Robbe-Grillet's playfulness. A passage from the novel describing a political poster could apply equally to the relationship between these allusions and the narrative: "Among the usual words some suspect term occasionally stands out like a signal, and the sentence it illuminates so equivocally seems for a moment to conceal many things, or nothing at all" (49). However, the novel's conclusion denies the meaninglessness—and the frivolousness—of the Oedipal content. Had Wallas acted differently, the Oedipal references *would* have meant nothing—except perhaps that Robbe-Grillet was trying to confuse readers or tempt us into outrageous interpretations. Because Wallas acts as he does, because he kills Dupont and fulfills the Oedipal role of the investigator who is himself the murderer, we can infer finally that the Oedipal allusions preceding that event are clues predicting it and that the action of *The Erasers* follows the basic pattern of *Oedipus the King*.

The allusions become, in effect, retroactive signals both to content (a murder) and form (the Oedipus myth). A retroactive signal is a paradox, which might seem simply like clever wordplay for explaining elements that other critics, such as Morrissette, have already accounted for. Nonetheless, this term reflects one of the conundrums of reading the novel and thus significantly focuses attention on the reader's part in *producing* the text. I will examine this point in more detail later, but its importance can be emphasized by looking at the final role that Morrissette proposes the Oedipus myth performs: that of psychiatric unifying principle.

In Robbe-Grillet's system, Morrissette suggests, individuals make certain objects the "supports" of their passions and thoughts; these objects become not "metaphoric talismans" but living embodiments of emotions (64). Consequently, Wallas' predisposition to *see* Oedipal objects, even though he never consciously identifies them as such, supplies the objective correlative for the Oedipus complex that guides him. Morrissette's description of Robbe-Grillet's system seems plausible; however, in claiming that Wallas is motivated by an Oedipus complex, he relies too heavily upon extraneous evidence. Such a Freudian interpretation of Wallas' behavior actually depends upon a faulty syllogism: if Wallas is a modern Oedipus and if he kills a man, then that man *must* be his father. This specious reasoning inspires Morrissette to reinterpret several actions in a psychoanalytic light, particularly Wallas' flirtation with Dupont's ex-wife, Evelyn, whom Morrissette identifies as Wallas' stepmother and, possibly, sister. Yet as Robert Brock observes, asking "how many clues can be found to 'prove' that Wallas was Dupont's son" is futile, "because in the end nothing of the kind is proven."[12] There is no concrete evidence that Wallas and Dupont are blood related, much less son and father.

But a mythic parallel need not be exact to be functional, and so there is no reason to rewrite the family histories of Robbe-Grillet's characters. Just because Wallas does not repeat every act or suffer every complication of Oedipus' life does not mean that he is any less an Oedipus figure. It is enough that he duplicates certain crucial acts of Oedipus' history—namely, that of the detective hunting down himself as the murderer; we do not have to force Wallas to commit patricide. But although Morrissette has psychoanalyzed Wallas on too little evidence, his proposal that the Oedipus myth operates on a psychoanalytic level, as well as on a structural one, deserves closer attention. To explain that possibility, let us take a second look at those ubiquitous Oedipal references.

Wallas, as Morrissette points out, perceives many objects and actions that seem blatantly Oedipal, yet he never specifies them as such. He is not alone in this obtuseness. Garanati, Evelyn Dupont, and Dr. Juard also confront or live among Oedipal signs but fail to make anything of them. Yet Wallas is the only character who seems "haunted" by these objects and situations and occasionally comes close to connecting them to the myth. For example, of the eraser he doggedly seeks, Wallas remembers both the number of syllables and the alphabetic composition of the middle syllable, but not what is possibly its brand name, Oedipus. At another time, he envisions himself in a Pompeian-style city, speaking in some official role to a crowd gathered in the forum before "a temple (or a theater, or something of the same kind)" (230). This memory, with physical details resembling the opening of *Oedipus the King*, "suddenly becomes quite piercing; for a fraction of a second, the entire scene assumes an extraordinary density" (230). The vision vanishes, but almost immediately thereafter Wallas remembers something he had forgotten: that the relative for whom he and his mother searched when he was a child was his father. Finally, Wallas encounters several "riddles" that he believes have some significance, but what that meaning is, he cannot tell. There is the chief commissioner's aphorism, "Sometimes you go through hell and high water to find a murderer far away when all you need to do is stretch out your hand" (197), which echoes like a refrain in Wallas' mind after he kills Dupont. And, of course, Wallas cannot remember the drunk's rendition of the Sphinx' riddle ("What animal is parricide in the morning, incestuous at noon, and blind at night" [226]), even though it worries him so much after the murder that he queries the drunk.

The name *Oedipus* lies just beneath Wallas' consciousness. His subconscious recognizes its importance, as his repeated attractions to the Oedipal and his obsessive efforts to locate the gum eraser demonstrate. For Wallas, the Oedipus myth is a sort of silent oracle predicting his destiny. Theoretically, if Wallas could hear and comprehend this oracle, he could prevent his own murder of Dupont. However, it is precisely Wallas' inability to connect Oedipal objects to the myth and then to his situation that *makes* him Oedipal. Like the Oedipus who reigned over Thebes for many years and who initiated the investigation into Laius' death, Wallas cannot see what is most necessary to see. During one of his several requests for the mysterious eraser, Wallas thinks there is a good reason why he cannot remember its brand, an ambiguous thought since, on the one hand, the eraser possibly does not exist but, on the other hand, were Wallas to remember this name, he would not be the Oedipal figure he is. In brief, the Oedipus myth is to Wallas as Oedipus' early life was to him; and the numerous references to the myth serve not only as retroactive signals to the climactic murder scene but also as a way to *represent* Wallas as a contemporary Oedipus and an antidetective. Wallas encounters the Oedipal just as Oedipus lived the first half of his life—without understanding it.

The crux of *The Erasers* may thus be identified as Wallas' ambivalence between assuming the role of the conventional detective or that of the young Oedipus. In his gathering of evidence, in his interrogations of witnesses, and in his theories about the crime, he approaches the former. But in his frequent digressive quests for the eraser, in his irrational feeling that if a conversation were important to his case he would be able to overhear it (178), and in his inability to recognize and collate the many clues revealing the past and prefiguring the future, he inclines toward the paranoia and blindness of the latter. When Wallas murders Dupont, he settles for good the question about roles. Dupont, as the murdered victim, has given birth to the detective Wallas, but Wallas subsequently kills Dupont and becomes the criminal Oedipus.

Wallas is, of course, an "arrested" Oedipus since he never attains the inner sight or understanding of the self-blinded Oedipus, since he never discovers how he came to do what he did. The self-blinding mytheme is thus conspicuously and significantly absent from Wallas' story. In fact, Wallas leaves the case almost as much in the dark as when he began it. If *The Erasers*—which erases the boundaries between victim, murderer, and detective and presents humans groping for clues and answers to reality—contains a central spokesperson, it is Fabius, the commissioner of the Bureau of Investigation. In his younger years, Fabius would have been the hero of a conventional detective story, but lately he has developed some ideas that have caused his subordinates, including Wallas, to doubt his competence: "Already people were saying that he mistrusted easy solutions, now it is whispered that he has ceased to believe in the existence of any solution whatever" (56). The world of *The Erasers* is the world imagined by Fabius. For the characters, there is no Solution, no Truth, no comprehensive understanding; Robbe-Grillet suggests that this is so because, when involved, we are always too close to the facts—or the facts are too close (relevant) to us—to see them.

The Oedipus myth therefore supplies the novel's central structure and also provides a means for expressing a metaphysics arrived at through extension of a psychoanalytic reality. The "complex" that guides Wallas is not the Freudian Oedipus complex strictly interpreted as the wish to possess the mother and destroy the father. Rather, it is the more general, somewhat self-destructive urge, which is part of the Oedipus complex, to repress those truths that might help us to control our destiny or at least to understand it. Only the reader, as a voyeur to many of the characters' thoughts and actions, knows how Wallas comes to be the criminal. This is by no means to slight the reader's role; quite the opposite. For besides presenting us with a world—unlike the worlds of traditional detective novels—that refuses to offer up all the clues to its mysteries, *The Erasers* also presents us with a text that asks us to participate in its making. In brief, Robbe-Grillet's novel challenges us to stop sitting back and watching as the detective cleverly pieces together the puzzle and, instead, to start piecing together a puzzle ourselves, that of the text.

Butor's *Passing Time*: Oedipus Revealed

Because the antidetective novel is vitally concerned with metaphysics, one way to understand this genre would be to plot each such novel's position on a continuum of metaphysical thought. In the case of *The Erasers* and *Passing Time*, the distance between two points is short. Butor's assessment of his novel sounds, in fact, like a more casual explanation of the metaphysics of *The Erasers*. In a 1974 interview he asserts that he cannot describe what "really happened in Bleston," for his novel depicts life, which, unlike the detective story, is full of "holes." As Butor concludes, we "always have to work in order to find reality."[13]

But if it is relatively simple to compare the metaphysics of *The Erasers* and of *Passing Time*, it seems more difficult to build a case that the latter is an antidetective story employing the Oedipus myth. For one thing, Jacques Revel, Butor's protagonist and narrator, is not a professional detective like Wallas; nor does he appear, at first, even to be an amateur like Pynchon's Oedipa Maas. He is a French businessman, hired for a year by the English firm of Matthews & Sons as a commercial translator, who begins a journal describing his stay in Bleston, England, because he wants to rescue his past (36), to deliver himself from lethargy (81), and to seek a meaning for his life (117). This approach and these motives would appear to group *Passing Time* with psychological novels like Max Frisch's *Homo Faber* or Alberto Moravia's *The Lie* more than with the antidetective narratives of Robbe-Grillet and Pynchon. Further, unlike *The Erasers*, where the Oedipus myth is never named but virtually shouts for recognition, in *Passing Time* Oedipus is mentioned but seems overshadowed as a mythic referent by the more prominent myths of Theseus and Cain.[14] With Revel pointing directly to his Theseus-like struggle to find his way in the labyrinthine city and to his Cain-like efforts at composing, we might easily overlook—or resist—the possibility that his situation could accommodate yet another mythic correspondence.

In fact, Revel himself is partly responsible for obscuring both the detective and the Oedipal features of his narrative. Many critics have noted that Revel's journal is strongly influenced by the detective story structure as expounded within the novel by George Burton, author of *The Murder of Bleston* and other mysteries. But most readers have missed the fact that Burton's definition also provides Revel with the perfect means to disguise, or at least to delay revealing, his primary reasons for writing and the true nature of his journal. Revel begins his journal on May 1, recounting throughout that month the activities of October, his first month in Bleston. By June, he decides that he cannot follow this strict chronological method and writes about the present as well as November. This decision seems inspired by a conversation he has with Burton on May 18 in which Burton asserts that the detective narrative "is not merely the projection on a flat surface of a series of events, it rebuilds these as it were spatially, since they appear differently according to the position occupied by the detective or by the narrator" (158). By July, Revel is relating the events of December, May, and July; by August, he is not only writing about the past and the present but also criticizing and correcting accounts written in May and June. This complicated tracking and backtracking continues until his last entry on September 30, the day he leaves Bleston.

Revel's narrative method suggests that he hopes to connect spatially the events of his life, as Burton maintains the detective novelist does. But in his eagerness to draw such connections, Revel often neglects to arrange events causally, as would a conventional detective solving a crime. In addition, his belief that the significance, and even the facts, of an event can change with time makes many of his conclusions suspect—or at least temporary. Readers are consequently forced not only to detect and assemble the facts, as they must do in reading Robbe-Grillet's multiple-viewpoint novel, but also to judge them. The most crucial fact to uncover is Revel's motive for beginning his journal. Ann Jefferson claims that "unlike a detective novel, there is no single event in [*Passing Time*] (like a murder) which provokes a coherent search for its origins."[15] To the contrary, it is precisely a "murder" and an investigation into its origins that lie at the heart of Revel's journal—and Butor's novel. Once we pinpoint this center, we also recognize that Revel's ultimate, and most important, mythic connection is to Oedipus.

Revel provides a number of reasons for writing, some of them already listed, including the need to find his way in "the labyrinth of [his] days in Bleston" (183). But Revel's changing view of his motives indicates that he cannot be trusted to name the true reason. The catalyst must be sought in the events that inspired his first journal entry. By adopting the narrative approach that he does, Revel is able to postpone describing April until chapter 4 (August), when we finally discover that on April 27, he burned his map of

Bleston, a symbolic murder of the town he believed, and still believes, is destroying him. On April 28, Revel had to buy a new map because he could not find his way around town; and on April 29, he realized the senselessness of his "crime," since the new map did not disguise the disappearance of the other but emphasized it (196). On the last day of April, Revel bought the paper for his journal. In other words, Revel's need to write is directly tied to his attempted murder of Bleston; it is first and foremost a need to investigate a crime. Here we find a pattern we know well: the criminal has turned detective and is seeking himself.

Revel's journal can thus be seen as a cat-and-mouse game in which the truth-seeking investigator attempts to flush out the criminal hiding in its pages. The self-defensive side of Revel would have us believe that the city of Bleston—wounded, but not mortally, by his burning of its image—has turned avenger and is persecuting him; and certainly one of the themes of *Passing Time* is that the modern industrial city gnaws away at the humanity of its citizens. However, Oedipus, too, was provoked by his victim, Laius, yet such provocation did not excuse him in the eyes of the gods or himself. We must not let the credibility of Revel's self-defense keep us from seeing that he himself is finally to blame for the misfortune plaguing him after he burns the map that represents the city.

The connection between this irrational act and Revel's misfortune might, in fact, be found in Burton's explanation of the detective's role. According to him, the detective must uncover the murderer in order to cleanse "this small fraction of the world" from the defilement that murder brings, that "deep-seated, age-old discord which becomes incarnate in the criminal" and whose primitive presence disturbs the established order (144). Hence, even if Revel's attempt to kill Bleston were born of the purest motives (which is questionable since he seems driven by hatred and by disgust at his own degradation), the effort ultimately contaminates him and his surroundings, just as Oedipus' patricide polluted him and Thebes. If Bleston has infected him, Revel has exacerbated that infection by turning murderer.

Seeing Revel's actions as the repetition of an age-old discord, in the manner of Oedipus' patricide, helps to clarify his behavior after he begins his journal, especially his part in George Burton's "accident." On July 11, Burton is knocked down, but not killed, by a car, a hit-and-run that almost everyone views as a bungled murder attempt. Revel blames himself, for he believes that by revealing Burton's true identity to James Jenkins on May 31 and then to the Bailey sisters the next evening, he made Burton an easy target of people angered by Burton's use of their family history in *The Murder of Bleston*. At first, Revel compares his situation to that of Theseus who killed his father out of negligence (171). In early August, he revises this conclusion, determining that the betrayal to the Bailey sisters was compelled by his desire to show off for Rose, whom he thought he loved. "I contrived," he admits, "to have my secret dragged from me; and I was well aware that I was endangering George Burton's life . . . , but I disregarded this, I turned murderer for the sake of Rose" (194). With this confession, Revel seems to insist that he never actively wished his friend's death but became an accomplice out of love, or self-promotion.

Yet love cannot account for the similar betrayal to Jenkins, nor can it illuminate Revel's actions just before Burton's "accident," when he contemplated burning Burton's photograph (138, 142), then considered throwing it into the river (142), and finally settled upon crumpling it in his fist "with instinctive fury" (143). Surely Revel was neither merely negligent nor an unwilling agent in Burton's accident but actively wished his death. Typically, he blames Bleston for forcing him to conspire against his friend, and yet his desire to burn Burton's photograph suggests a different catalyst—a catalyst that is also implied in a dream he had the night he burned the Bleston map. In this dream, Revel, Lucien Blaise, and the Burtons watched as their rum-soaked copies of *The Murder of Bleston* burned, the flames destroying first, "the seven letters of the word Bleston," and then the author's name, "J. C. Hamilton" (Burton's pseudonym) (199). The second near murder is obviously born of the first. For some unexplained reason, Revel wants to eliminate not only Bleston but also George Burton.

As in *Oedipus the King*, with its slow movement from concealment to consciousness, Revel approaches self-knowledge only gradually. After learning of Rose's engagement to Lucien and assuming that he has lost her for good, he rereads parts of his journal, concluding that these accounts appeared "more and more like the scrupulous work of another to whom I had confided only a portion of my secrets, through a lack of time, through incapacity to distinguish as yet what was important, and also, I must admit, through a desire to deceive that other, to deceive myself" (191). Revel follows this confession with a deliberate attempt at rectification. He describes for the first time his burning of the map and also admits that he divulged Burton's identity to the Baileys in the hope of impressing Rose.

At the end of August, when Revel also loses Ann Bailey, the detective side of his personality casts out other masks and scapegoats behind which the criminal side has hidden. In an Oedipal resolution, he declares, "I should have liked to burn out my eyes which had only served to deceive me, my eyes and all these pages I have written" (244). Revel resists this impulse, but the denouement of his story is nonetheless Oedipal. "The pattern is complete," he states, "and I am left out of it" (250), a conclusion that recalls Burton's idea that the detective abolishes all errors, ignorances, and lies so that the actors may regroup themselves in "a new pattern from which one member [the criminal] is automatically excluded" (144). Having at last detected and confronted the criminal within, Revel can admit responsibility for Burton's accident. He even acknowledges that he will retain his share of complicity regardless of whether Jenkins is involved (260).

The losses of Rose and Ann move Revel toward self-(revel)ation. With each loss he realizes that he has deceived himself about the relationship, and these realizations subsequently seem to encourage him to uncover other self-deceptions. Significantly, Revel insists that part of the reason why he lost these women is that he devoted time to his journal rather than to them. Revel has been consumed by his investigation either because he subconsciously recognized its real purpose or because he wanted to escape from social or emotional commitments. These inferences lead, in turn, to others: (1) Revel fears women or relationships; (2) he has subconsciously used his journal to punish himself for his criminal activities; and (3) he is aware of his criminal nature and either wishes to protect others from it or worries that contact with others will force him to confront that dark side. None of these possibilities can be definitely proved, but their number alone reveals the complexity of Revel and his story. About all one can safely say is that each movement toward the truth seems wrested from Revel, as it was from Oedipus, and that, as is the case with *The Erasers*, readers can never know everything about Revel or his time in Bleston.

Revel's view of the truth may be more relative than that of Oedipus, and his self-revelations may lack the other's conviction, but he at least seems to go beyond being merely mystified—where Wallas ends—and to approach the mystical, in the manner of Oedipus in *Oedipus at Colonus*. By identifying, sentencing, and punishing himself for his transgressions, Revel appears to have gained some of Oedipus' inner sight and special status. During his Oedipal exile, Revel believes that Bleston has chosen him to be its prophet of doom. He spends his last days in the city learning as much as possible about its streets and sites so as to inform the world that Bleston—and its inhabitants— wants to die. The surreptitious map burning that precipitated Revel's quest for the truth about himself is replaced, finally, by his prophecy of an actual holocaust, an event that will perhaps precipitate a quest for a better world (267).

But although Revel's actions at the end of the novel link him with the self-blinded Oedipus of *Oedipus at Colonus*, the integral structure of *Passing Time* is provided by the three mythemes that comprise the central action of *Oedipus the King*. Once this structure is recognized, not only does the general movement of the novel become clearer, but many of Revel's actions are also illuminated. Like Oedipus, and unlike the conventional detective, Revel does not solve the case by rationally piecing together the facts; in fact, he does not know what "the facts" really are. Instead, he leaves the country, like Oedipus, with only a solitary awareness: that, regardless of his motives and "the facts," he is a guilty man.

Pynchon's *The Crying of Lot 49*: Oedipus in Suburbia

If in Wallas we meet a character who sees reality as if through a dark glass and in Revel we find a man whose view of reality becomes clearer but never perfect, in Pynchon's Oedipa Maas we confront a protagonist who loses sight of reality almost completely. Not only does Pynchon's heroine discover a metaphysical void where Robbe-Grillet's and Butor's heroes face merely a metaphysical quagmire, but readers of *The Crying of Lot 49* must also learn to live with even fewer absolutes than must readers of *The Erasers* and *Passing Time*. As Peter Cooper puts it, "Like Oedipa, the reader encounters 'a secret richness and concealed density of dream' but nothing much more concrete and verifiable."[16]

The Crying of Lot 49 is constructed out of the same triad of Oedipal mythemes forming Robbe-Grillet's and Butor's novels. However, this construction has not been obvious to all readers, for critics have argued since Pynchon's novel was published in 1966 about whether Oedipa is Oedipal. A common position has been that, in naming Oedipa, Pynchon is poking fun at a literary convention that requires meaningfulness from characters' names when real life demands no such correspondence. As Tony Tanner suggests, the wild names that Pynchon gives his characters are "a gesture against the tyranny of naming itself."[17] But even if we were to agree that this is Pynchon's point—and I do not think we should—the only way to reach this conclusion is by responding conventionally and seeking further evidence of the Oedipus myth. As in *The Erasers*, the myth hangs over Pynchon's novel like a perplexing clue, waiting to be confirmed or denied. With the very first sentence—"One summer afternoon Mrs Oedipa Maas came home"[18]—Pynchon turns readers into amateur detectives, just as Pierce Inverarity turns Oedipa into a detective in the opening scene. Our mystery is to learn how to read this story.

Edward Mendelson provides an accurate description of the relationship between Oedipa's quest and Oedipus' history when he states that Oedipa's name "refers back to the Sophoclean Oedipus who begins his search for the solution of a problem (a problem, like Oedipa's, involving a dead man) as an almost detached observer, only to discover how deeply implicated he is in what he finds."[19] Clearly, this correlation between Oedipa and Oedipus contains gaps, as did the correlations between Wallas and Oedipus, and Revel and Oedipus. For one, Oedipa searches not for a murderer but for the meaning and the nature of a secret organization named the Tristero. For another, the crimes of patricide and incest have nothing to do with her self-incrimination. Finally, her investigation ends by accusing herself not of committing unnatural acts against her parents but of failing to live an engaged life. However, as for Wallas and Revel, such differences are incidental. As a brief overview of Oedipa's adventures will show, her experience is essentially that of Oedipus: an interrogation of a mystery in the world leads to a self-interrogation, which results, finally, in a revised understanding of both the world and oneself.

When Oedipa arrives in San Narciso to meet Metzger, her coexecutor and special counsel to Inverarity's estate, she has a sort of Sherlock Holmesian view of the world, as if its phenomena were only waiting for someone with a colossal magnifying glass to detect them and read their meaning. Upon first seeing the city, she compares it to the circuit card of a transistor radio she once dismantled and concludes: "There were to both outward patterns a hieroglyphic sense of concealed meaning, of an intent to communicate. There'd seemed no limit to what the printed circuit could have told her (if she had tried to find out); so in her first minute of San Narciso, a revelation also trembled just past the threshold of her understanding" (13). Appropriately, when Oedipa initially thinks she has uncovered evidence of an underground postal system—first on the stamp of a letter from her husband, Mucho, and then through Mike Fallopian, a patron of the Scope bar—she assumes that "like the private eye in any long-ago radio drama" all she would need to solve its mystery were "grit, resourcefulness, exemption from hidebound cops' rules" (91).

Oedipa approaches the mystery of the Tristero as if it were a wonderful chance for her to play detective. Like Oedipus seeking Laius' murderer, she is certain that she will find the answer, and also like her namesake, she never imagines that it is her view of the world that is actually under investigation. Yet as each private eye task that she puts into practice fails—her witnesses die, disappear, or simply complicate the mystery; her clues never gel into positive evidence; her theories refuse to turn into solutions—Oedipa grows to doubt that she will share in the "revelation in progress all around her" (28) and, finally, that she will ever again be able to distinguish reality.

The point is that Oedipa's view of reality was a false one. The more accurate view involves uncertainty and is, therefore, more perilous because it not only undermines her former comfortable view but also threatens to destroy everything she believed about herself and the world. As Oedipa nears the edge of this void, she hesitates, having become "anxious that her revelation not expand beyond a certain point. Lest, possibly, it grow larger than she and assume her to itself" (125). She feels reluctant about following up anything and goes to absurd lengths to avoid talking about Randolph Driblette (124–25), the director of *The Courier's Tragedy,* who committed suicide soon after Oedipa attended his production and questioned him about the Tristero.

Like Oedipus, however, she takes that perilous plunge and surfaces with terrifying knowledge. Isolated, alienated, and frightened, Oedipa must face the possibility that the only conclusion is an indeterminate one that does not solve the mystery but reaffirms it: the Tristero exists, or she is fantasizing its existence, or she is the victim of an elaborate plot, or she is imagining such a plot, in which case she is insane (128). Having experienced the void, Oedipa responds in a typically Oedipal way. She drives on the freeway at night for a while with her headlights off (132), her version of self-blinding. But nothing happens, and so Oedipa, unlike Oedipus, finds no outlet through which to disperse the horror of her revelation. She is forced to accept the position that although she may wait for an answer, she will probably never know.

In revising her view of the world, Oedipa comes to understand that her former life, a carbon copy of the lives of most middle-class Americans, was a sick life. The security of the suburbs has meant conformity, callousness, and near-paralysis: "She had heard all about excluded middles; they were bad shit, to be avoided; and how had it ever happened here [in America], with the chances once so good for diversity?" (136). One even suspects that Oedipa might now discern that the revelation that eluded her upon first glimpsing San Narciso was actually implicit in her generalized description of the place: "Like many named places in California it was less an identifiable city than a grouping of concepts—census tracts, special purpose bond-issue districts, shopping nuclei, all overlaid with access roads to its own freeway" (12). This is an America to which Oedipa cannot return; indeed, "the only way she could continue, and manage to be at all revelant to it, was as an alien, unfurrowed, assumed full circle into some paranoia" (137).

As Stefano Tani observes, *The Crying of Lot 49* contains a structural nonsolution (the open-endedness) and an emotional solution (Oedipa's growth to maturity and compassion). In addition, like Oedipa, readers will never know the Tristero's true nature nor will we know what happens at the auction where Inverarity's stamp collection is being sold—although some have been compelled to hypothesize.[20] To read the text is to accept its mystery; in interpreting it, we must adopt Oedipa's indeterminate perspective. To put this another way, Pynchon's novel sets up a hermeneutic hall of mirrors: our interpretive quest is mirrored in Oedipa's, whose similar quest is mirrored in Oedipus'. In each case, knowledge replaces ignorance, but this knowledge is tentative and temporary. As with Robbe-Grillet's *The Erasers* and Butor's *Passing Time*, the mystery novel has become not only a story about a mystery but also a mystery itself.

Oedipus as Antidetective

In order to agree that both Oedipa and the reader move from certainty to uncertainty, a direction exactly opposite that of detectives and readers in the conventional detective novel, critics such as James Dean Young and Terry Caesar have argued that we must abandon the idea that Oedipa is an Oedipal figure.[21] As I mentioned early in this chapter, Oedipus' self-blinding suggests that he has cleared up, beyond doubt, the mystery of Laius' murder as well as the mystery of his past. "Alas! All out! All known, no more conceal-ment!" he cries. "O Light! May I never look on you again, / Revealed as I am, sinful in my begetting, / Sinful in marriage, sinful in shedding of blood!" (58). The oracle has proved true, and Oedipus has proven its truth. How far this ending seems from Oedipa's directionless stumbling toward the position that the only certainty is uncertainty, that the only truth is indeterminacy. How far Oedipus' discovery also seems from the relativism found in Robbe-Grillet's and Butor's novels.

But this conventional interpretation of Oedipus' end deserves another look. What we are forgetting in imagining this disparity is that the truth is not revealed to Oedipus as it was, say, to Moses, nor did Oedipus agree to his Fate as did Faust when he signed his soul over to the Devil.[22] Like Wallas, Revel, and Oedipa, Oedipus has to seek knowledge, and in doing so he learns that those truths that seemed absolute were illusions. He is not a dutiful son but a patricide; he gained his throne not simply by his intelligence but also by his crime; his love has been unnatural; and he has been blind when he thought he saw perfectly. In short, Oedipus discovers that the knowledge he believed the most unequivocal was actually the most equivocal.

Thus, even though Oedipus determines that the evidence against him is conclusive, the ending and general movement of his life imply a more uncertain position. The ambiguity of truth is emphasized in Oedipus' exile from Thebes, when he, who counted himself the most miserable of men, is exalted by the gods. In this exaltation, Oedipus reveals that he has learned the lesson that what is true today might not be so tomorrow. He tells Theseus: "Be sure you cannot fail of your reward / In giving Oedipus this dwelling-place / *Unless heaven means to play him false again*" (*Oedipus at Colonus* 90, italics mine). Oedipus now understands that to be human means to lack total vision, absolute knowledge; the gods, and reality, may turn on him at any time.

The view that Sophocles' Oedipus discovers the limits of human knowledge receives historical support from several philosophers of ancient Greece. R. G. A. Buxton notes that "Gorgias affirmed that the foundations of human knowledge were shaky. Protagoras insisted on the ἀδηλότης, lack of clarity, which affected men's knowledge of one major aspect of the world—divinity." As Buxton concludes, "Man might be the measure of all things, but his insight was, at least in one respect, severely limited."[23]

Buxton maintains that Sophocles was consistently concerned with this theme of limited human knowledge: "The plays of Sophokles and the pronouncements of Delphi alike convey a sense of the inscrutability of the gods, and of man's inability fully to grasp their will in time to avert disaster."[24] E. R. Dodds states the case more fully for *Oedipus the King*, supporting the notion that the overall view of reality, especially as expressed by the tragedy's conclusion, is one of nonassurance more than assurance. Oedipus gropes, Dodds writes, as every person must grope, "not knowing who he is or what he has to suffer: we all live in a world of appearances which hides from us who-knows-what dreadful reality." But Oedipus also pursues the truth, seeking to solve every riddle, "even the riddle to which the answer is that human happiness is built on an illusion."[25]

These observations also apply to the stories of Wallas, Revel, and Oedipa but with some important modifications. For one, whereas Oedipus remains insatiable in his quest, these twentieth-century investigators occasionally lose their appetite for the pursuit. In general, they are not less enthusiastic, just less certain about how to proceed and about whether their efforts will be rewarded with any kind of knowledge at all. This is a difference that probably *can* be attributed to the distance between a religious world and a nonreligious one. Simply by their presence, the gods reassured Sophoclean audiences, and Oedipus, that final knowledge does exist, even though humans might be unable to reach it. Wallas, Revel, Oedipa, and many modern readers cannot presume even this much possibility. As Tani observes, and as I noted in chapter 3, in this century we have replaced the assumption that science can explain the mystery of the universe with the acceptance that science will raise further mysteries, increasing the gap between the known and the unknown (109–10).

Another significant difference between Sophocles' version of the Oedipus myth and the postmodern antidetective story lies with the effect each has on its audience. Greek viewers of Sophocles' drama left the theatre with Oedipus' knowledge; indeed, most brought that knowledge to the performance. Their attention was primarily held by following Oedipus' struggle to arrive at that knowledge. However, readers of the antidetective narrative must labor as hard as the detective and often must labor against the detective to discover the truth. Even the most energetic effort is no guarantee that we will come any closer to solving the mystery *within* the text than does the antidetective; in fact, although we can solve the mystery *of* the text by finding a way to resolve into meaning its various components, including its use of the Oedipus myth, such a resolution remains tentative, not final. For what we learn from Wallas, Revel, Oedipa—and Oedipus—is that meaning does not inhere in an action or an object but is a projection of the interpreter, and this projection can change as the interpreter changes the position from which he or she views the facts or revises the facts themselves. What we believe the text to say today, we may not believe tomorrow.

But despite these differences between Sophocles' Oedipus myth and the antidetective story using that myth, *Oedipus the King* is obviously more closely related to this postmodern form than it is to the classical detective story to which it is most frequently compared. As three influential fiction writers of the postmodern era have realized, its structure is intrinsically antidetective. Because of this structure, Tani is surely wrong to claim that the Oedipus myth—along with the existential quest, the duality of detective and criminal, the concept of time, and latent irrationality—is *one* element of antidetective fiction. Rather, the myth encompasses these other components: Oedipus' investigation turns into a search for his origins; Oedipus discovers that he is the murderer he seeks; time is telescoped and virtually erased when Oedipus learns that his future was determined years ago; and what Oedipus finds out about himself in a day is so incredible that it borders on the absurd.

Ironically, then, the play that Aristotle chose as the nearly flawless example of the causal plot has become a source for a postmodern genre that seeks to sabotage such seamless teleology. And the Greek hero who is frequently viewed as the investigator who pursues the truth no matter what the cost has become the prototype for postmodern investigators and readers, who discover that the cost of pursuing the truth is finding out that it cannot be fully or finally known.

C H A P T E R 5

Reading Myths and Mythemes after Freud: From Oedipal Incest to Oedipal Insight

■

When Sigmund Freud chose the Oedipus myth to exemplify his theory of infant development, he changed forever the way we look at the myth and the way we might read myths in general. No longer simply a tale about the stranger's winning of the princess, the hero's fight with the dragon, or the king's effort to save a dying land, the Oedipus myth was now a psychological drama about desire or, perhaps more accurately, a drama about the psychology of desire.[1] Equally important, such a reading paved the way for similar readings of other myths, providing a means for (apparently) penetrating through every myth's surface story to the unconscious unknown that the myth expresses. That psychoanalysis has not closed the ontological gap between event and meaning that makes a myth mythic but has in fact multiplied the number of theories regarding that gap is more a testimony to myth's power than a sign of the inadequacy of psychoanalytic readings. Psychoanalysis thus gave us principles and methods for reading myths but also an (apparently) endless history of oppositional readings of these myths.

Probably the most famous history of these oppositional readings is that surrounding the Oedipus myth (although the history surrounding the Narcissus myth runs a close second). From the moment Freud appropriated the myth, Oedipus became indelibly tied to psychoanalysis—and to desire. It would therefore be impossible to trace the career of the Oedipus myth in twentieth-century fiction without examining stories in which desire is a central component. But because Freud's ideas about family dynamics and individual psychology have been contested throughout this century, in turning to such stories, we are not automatically fixated on Oedipal triangles and complexes. A number of critics—from Freud's colleagues, Carl Jung and Alfred Adler, to feminists such as Simone de Beauvoir and Nancy Chodorow, to Marxists such as Gilles Deleuze and Félix Guattari—have formed a discordant chorus of opposition to Freud's theories of the family, and typically they have worked out this opposition within the Oedipus myth.[2] This return to the myth, which might best be described as a rereading of Oedipus' history with or via Freud, has not only enlarged the semantic encyclopedias of the incest and patricide mythemes, the cornerstones of the Oedipus complex,[3] it has also attempted to relocate the myth's place in psychoanalytic theory and twentieth-century thought. Consequently, although the Oedipus myth may always remain within the domain of psychoanalysis, it has not remained under the dominion of Freud.

André Green points out that whether or not Freud read Sophocles' drama correctly matters less than "what he taught us to seek behind the myth: the repression of the unconscious."[4] This inference refers to Freud's observation that *Oedipus the King* develops like a psychoanalytic session: "The action of the play consists in nothing other than the process of revealing, with cunning delays and ever-mounting excitement—a process that can be likened to the work of a psychoanalysis—that Oedipus himself is the murderer of Laïus, but further that he is the son of the murdered man and of Jocasta."[5] Hence, while some critics have quibbled over the validity of naming a complex about infantile wishes after a man who comes to know his parents late in life,[6] others have been more interested in the implication that Oedipus knew he was making a mistake at the crossroads and in the royal bed but that he hid, repressed, or censored that knowledge.

This interest has developed along many lines of reasoning, from the view that Oedipus deliberately withholds the truth to the position that he engages in some kind of self-deception, be it repression or avoidance. This approach to the myth reveals itself in the work of many different groups, not only psychoanalysts (such as Jacques Lacan and Peter Rudnytsky), but also classical scholars (such as Philip Vellacott), literary critics (such as Morton Kaplan and Robert

Kloss), and fiction writers. While their positions differ, sometimes significantly,[7] each of these groups makes the point that Oedipus somehow hid the truth about himself *from* himself.

For example, Jacques Lacan adheres to the traditional view that sees Oedipus as being ignorant of his crimes until his investigation into Laius' murder reveals the truth. However, Lacan emphasizes that Oedipus *knows* the answer to his own question—Who (or what) am I? Truth consists not of knowledge, but of recognition. So central is Oedipus' movement from *méconnaissance* (misrecognition or mis-apprehension of one's own history) to *reconnaissance* (recognition) that Lacan posits it as a paradigm for the psychoanalytic situation.[8] The essential shift from Freud's focus is made evident in the following passage from Lacan's *Le Séminaire, livre II: Le Moi dans la théorie de Freud et dans la technique psychoanalytique*:

> The subject's question in no way refers to the results of any specific weaning, abandonment, or vital lack of love or affection; it concerns the subject's history inasmuch as the subject misapprehends, *misrecognizes*, it; this is what the subject's actual conduct is expressing in spite of himself, insofar as he obscurely seeks to *recognize* this history. His life is guided by a problematics which is not that of his life experience, but that of his destiny—that is, what is the meaning, the significance, of his history? What does his life story mean?[9]

In short, Freud justifies Oedipus' presence in psychoanalysis by emphasizing his crimes; Lacan focuses as much, if not more, on the nature of Oedipus' personal search for the truth about his history.[10]

Lacan's concentration on Oedipus' naming of the repressed or censored knowledge aligns him with others in his discipline—such as Rudnytsky—and literary critics such as Kaplan and Kloss[11]—all of whom stress Oedipus' knowledge in relation to his ignorance. This same emphasis appears in some relatively recent novels: Flannery O'Connor's *Wise Blood* (1952), Max Frisch's *Homo Faber* (1957), and Alberto Moravia's *The Lie* (1965). Each of these works suggests that the meaning of Oedipus' life is not so much *who* he killed or married but *how* he avoided the truth for so long. Although we cannot prove that in writing their stories these three authors drew upon or even knew the theories of contemporary psychoanalysis, their rendering of the Oedipus myth corresponds to the views of Lacan and Rudnytsky. Such a convergence of viewpoints seems to suggest that the extensive return to the myth initiated in response to Freud has led different kinds of readers to a similar position. No longer are we solely absorbed with Oedipus' status as an emblem of the main infantile conflict; our attention is now centered on the workings of Oedipus' mind. Desire need not be familial, but it must be unfamiliar. To signal this changed perspective, both analysts and writers are accentuating Oedipal mythemes other than or in addition to the ones of incest and patricide, the most important additions being the self-incrimination mytheme (15) and the self-blinding mytheme (17).

This return to the Oedipus myth is similar to that traced in the preceding chapter—in both cases our understanding of the myth has been enlarged—but with one important difference. In chapter 4 the return took place at the level of structure, as we measured one genre against another and, as a result, reclassified *Oedipus the King*. Here the return has been initiated at the level of content or, perhaps more accurately, *below* the level of content—the level of the unconscious. To put this another way, in the preceding chapter, our investigation was guided by a critical construct: genre. In this chapter, we are directed by the principles and methods of a discipline: psychoanalysis.

In fact, we can thank Freud not only for precipitating this return to the myth but also for providing the means to displace his reading of it. Freud himself declared that the poets and philosophers before him discovered the unconscious; he simply discovered the scientific method by which it could be studied.[12] While this does not mean that we need to psychoanalyze Oedipus in order to understand him, it does mean that we are more inclined than a pre-Freudian audience to view Oedipus' ignorance in terms of his unconscious and to see his anagnorisis as a surfacing of the repressed desire.

O'Connor's Haze Motes: An Oedipus *malgré lui*

We find a good example of the post-Freudian repositioning of interest in Oedipus' psychology in Flannery O'Connor's revisions of *Wise Blood*. Stuart Burns argues that in composing this novel O'Connor reduced the story's emphasis on Haze Motes' love for his mother and developed instead his struggle with his inherent spirituality.[13] According to Burns, in the five early short stories from which O'Connor drew *Wise Blood*, the religious obsession of the main character—who became Haze—is tied up with his Oedipus conflict. However, in *Wise Blood*, Haze's "need for Christ" and his fight against this need arise from his innate religiosity. Burns suggests that, despite O'Connor's revisions, the novel still exhibits vestiges of the Freudian sublimation;[14] and at least one reader has claimed that the story contains more than a trace of the Oedipus complex.[15] Nevertheless, a close study of *Wise Blood* reveals that the Oedipus myth, not the Oedipus complex, is the principal informing agent of the character of Haze Motes and that O'Connor's use of the myth reflects the paradigm shift outlined above.

The key scene for determining just how far an Oedipus complex motivates Haze is his visit at age ten to a carnival, followed by a meeting with his mother at home. At the carnival, Haze's father left him alone while his father entered a tent advertised as "SINsational" and "EXclusive." Knowing that his mother (who along with his evangelical grandfather had taught him Christian principles) "wouldn't want me in there," Haze bartered his way inside anyway. There he saw the "sinsation": a naked woman lying in a coffin. Back home, Haze was watched by his mother until he hid behind a tree, where he imagined her as the carnival woman in the casket. When his mother asked what he had seen, he did not answer. "Jesus died to redeem you," she said. Haze replied, "I never ast him." After that, "he forgot the guilt of the tent for the nameless unplaced guilt that was in him." The next day Haze secretly filled his shoes with rocks and walked a mile, thinking, "that ought to satisfy Him." But nothing happened, even though he looked for an omen: "If a stone had fallen he would have taken it as a sign." Still, he walked a half-mile more before he removed the shoes (37–39).

90

Certainly readers are justified in connecting Haze's "nameless unplaced guilt" to his vision of his mother in the casket, a vision that links sex and death. As Thomas LeClair notes, Haze never stops associating sex with his mother; all the women he takes up with display some of her habits of dress and some of her characteristics.[16] However, the sins that Haze hopes to expiate by punishing himself also include blasphemy. He seeks forgiveness as much for denying Christ's sacrifice ("I never ast him") as for seeing unclean sights and thinking unclean thoughts. It makes as much sense, then, to claim that Haze's mother gains a strong hold over his imagination because she speaks for the religion that obsesses him as it does to claim that she is sexually attractive to him. In fact, it makes more sense, since Haze's grandfather, a similar proselytizer of Christianity, also pervades his thoughts and reappears symbolically in the men he relates to.[17] With these two relationships, O'Connor takes great care to portray Haze as a "Christian *malgré lui*" (8), not a neurotic. And a primary way she achieves this portrayal is to associate Haze's progress from ignorance to insight with Oedipus—although to claim that O'Connor uses a pagan myth to advance a Christian theme might make her Christianity seem unorthodox.

Haze's central conflict concerns the matter of Faith. As a young boy, he

> didn't need to hear [his grandfather's preaching]. There was already a deep black wordless conviction in him that the way to avoid Jesus was to avoid sin. He knew by the time he was twelve years old that he was going to be a preacher. Later he saw Jesus move from tree to tree in the back of his mind, a wild ragged figure motioning him to turn around and come off into the dark where he was not sure of his footing, where he might be walking on the water and not know it and then suddenly know it and drown. Where he wanted to stay was in Eastrod with his two eyes open, and his hands always handling the familiar thing, his feet on the known track, and his tongue not too loose. (16)

This passage reveals two essential things about Haze. First, like Oedipus, he has a destiny that he cannot escape (mytheme 5): his character is immanently religious. Indeed, Haze's silent conviction that the Christian viewpoint must include sin shows an instinct beyond his years. As O'Connor explained to a friend, "Part of the mystery of existence is sin. When we think about the Crucifixtion [sic], we miss the point of it if we don't think about sin."[18]

Furthermore, just as Oedipus' lameness identified his true self, so Haze's clothing and demeanor expose his. Even after he renounces Christianity and starts believing in nothing and preaching the Church Without Christ, Haze continues to be marked by his fate. From the moment he arrives in Taulkinham, he is constantly mistaken for a preacher. The taxi driver is the first to make this mistake, saying that besides Haze's hat, there is "a look in [his] face somewheres" that gives him a preacherly appearance (21). Asa Hawks tells Haze, "Some preacher has left his mark on you" (32); Enoch Emery declares, "I knew when I first seen you you didn't have nobody nor nothing but Jesus" (36); Leora Watts exclaims at his "Jesus-seeing hat" (37); and Hoover Shoats states that when he first saw Haze he thought of Christ and Abraham Lincoln (86). When Haze purposely runs down his alter ego, Solace Layfield, with his car, Layfield attempts to confess his sins to Haze before dying (111). No matter how much Haze denies his destiny, he cannot rid himself of its stigmata, on either his body or in his head (the figure of Jesus moving in the back of his mind).

The second crucial fact disclosed in the biographical passage quoted above is that, like Oedipus, Haze will grow up to reject his fate and attempt to escape it. His desire to immure himself in Eastrod, safe from Jesus' request to follow him into the unknown, shows that Haze has not yet understood the true sacrifice required for Belief. In his penance for his actions at the carnival and after, we have seen that Haze awaits some sign that the Divine exists. By this, O'Connor suggests that Haze's religious commitment is tied too much to his intellect and not enough to his soul. Unsurprisingly, when this commitment is tested, it fails. In the army, his first time away from home, Haze cannot defend his religious stance and spends his remaining military service *studying* his soul and assuring himself that it is not there (18, italics mine). Later he builds his gospel for the Church Without Christ upon the idea that "it was not right to believe anything you couldn't see or hold in your hands or test with your teeth" (112). In O'Connor's world, however, Faith cannot be put under the microscope, for that is to contradict the meaning of the leap. Despite his naturally spiritual character, Haze has yet to grasp the elemental equation that Faith is faith.

Haze's flight from Jesus is, therefore, a flight from himself. But the means he chooses as his escape, the automobile, finally brings him back to himself. He believes that the car is "something that moved fast, in privacy, to the place you wanted to be" (101). Yet the more he drives, the less ground he seems to cover (112). As O'Connor puts it, Haze's car is a "death-in-life symbol."[19] It cannot take him to the one place he needs to go, that place in the back of his mind where Jesus moves from tree to tree. When a policeman pushes Haze's car over an embankment, Haze seems to realize this, as if the destruction of that immobile vehicle blasts open the door to that inner room: "Haze stood for a few minutes, looking over at the scene. His face seemed to reflect the entire distance across the clearing and on beyond, the entire distance that extended from his eyes to the blank gray sky that went on, depth after depth, into space. His knees bent under him and he sat down on the edge of the embankment with his feet hanging over" (113–14).[20]

Haze moves, in Lacan's terms, from *méconnaissance*—a misunderstanding of his authentic being—to *reconnaissance*—a realization of the truth. His realization corresponds to Oedipus' similar realization not in its particulars but in its application. Like Oedipus, Haze has been deceived by his senses: when he thought he saw perfectly, he was actually blind, and when he thought he was free of his fate, he had actually run head-on into it. These perceptions lead Haze to the Oedipal act of self-blinding—an act that O'Connor describes as a "life-in-death symbol."[21] The Oedipal connection materializes fully when Haze tells his landlady that he hopes people are blind when they are dead, because "if there's no bottom in your eyes, they hold more" (121).

In his introduction to O'Connor's *Everything That Rises Must Converge*, Robert Fitzgerald recalls that when writing *Wise Blood*,

O'Connor "reached an impasse with Haze and didn't know how to finish him off." Meanwhile, she read Sophocles' Theban plays and decided "to end her story with the self-blinding of Motes," reworking "the body of the novel to prepare for it."[22] O'Connor, who was living with the Fitzgeralds at the time, must have felt it was a happy coincidence—or divine intervention—that the publication of Fitzgerald's translation of Sophocles, the version she read, concurred with her impasse; for, ironically, in the pagan Oedipus she found a consummate prototype for her Christian *malgré lui*. Oedipus' history reveals the futility of attempting to evade a fate marked out by a higher power, of denying the truth about oneself, and of relying on one's senses to apprehend reality. These were exactly the points O'Connor was trying to make from a Christian perspective in *Wise Blood*.

Frisch's *Homo Faber*: Man the Masker

Although Walter Faber of Max Frisch's *Homo Faber* would not be caught dead in the same novel with Haze Motes, he resembles O'Connor's protagonist in a number of ways. First, just as Haze denied his real self, so Faber "unwittingly seeks to deceive himself regarding his true nature."[23] Second, Faber achieves this self-deception by consecrating technology and an empirical view of the world. Like Haze, he even has a special attachment to the automobile: "I'm used to working or driving my car," he states, "it's no holiday for me if there's no mechanism running" (76). Finally, Faber is eventually confronted by so many facts that he cannot help but discover "the prejudices and limitations of his feelings,"[24] the myopia of his conscious mind. Combined, these correspondences amount for both men to a movement from *méconnaissance* to *reconnaissance*—a movement that for Faber, as for Haze, is conveyed through various Oedipal mythemes.

A crucial difference between Faber's and Haze's stories is that Faber tells his himself, whereas Haze's is told by an unnamed third-person narrator. In *Wise Blood*, we gain access to Haze's unconscious by identifying the contradictions between what Haze says and what he does. But in a first-person narrative such as *Homo Faber*, the story exists as much between the lines as in them. In fact, we are not the only ones to find contradictions in Faber's tale. As Michael Butler observes, Faber himself finally takes part in this self-exposure: "The fundamental irony of his report is that Faber's language *catches him out*, i.e. the discrepancy between what he says and what he thinks he says becomes increasingly evident, until the point is reached when he himself can no longer overlook it."[25] The idea that a speaker's discourse provides entry to his or her unconscious returns us to Freud—whose analyses of dreams, jokes, and verbal slips demonstrate this point—and to Lacan, who takes this idea a step beyond Freud by staking the entire psychoanalytic situation in the connection between the unconscious and language.

Lacan's famous formula states that the unconscious is the discourse of the Other.[26] In Sophocles' play, he claims, this discourse finds literal embodiment in the oracle.

> Oedipus' unconscious is nothing other than this fundamental discourse whereby, long since, for all time, Oedipus' history is out there—written, and we know it, but Oedipus is ignorant of it, even as he is played out by it since the beginning. This goes way back—remember how the Oracle frightens his parents, and how he is consequently exposed, rejected. Everything takes place in function of the Oracle and of the fact that Oedipus is truly other than what he realizes as his history—he is the son of Laius and Jocasta, and he starts out his life ignorant of this fact. The whole pulsation of the drama of his destiny, from the beginning to the end, hinges on the veiling of this discourse, which is his reality without his knowing it.[27]

As Shoshana Felman observes, Lacan sees Oedipus' recognition of the truth as being radically tied up with language; it is essentially a speech act by which he "recognizes, and performatively names, his desire and his history (insofar as the misapprehension of the one has structured the other)."[28] For Lacan, "the nature of the efficacious action of analysis" is to bring the subject "to recognize and to name his desire." But, he continues, "it is not a question of recognizing something that would have already been there—a given—ready to be captured. In naming it, the subject creates, gives rise to something new, makes something new present in the world."[29]

Although written discourse is not identical to speech, it can perform the same revelatory function, especially when expressed in the informal, freethinking style of a journal or a diary. Lacan's description of the analytic action and his extension of it to *Oedipus the King* can thus provide a framework for understanding autobiographical fiction such as *Homo Faber* where the narrator writes to explain, defend, or simply relate his actions but instead exposes himself *to himself* and thereby reaches greater self-knowledge. A story that works in much the same way is Michel Butor's *Passing Time*, discussed as an antidetective novel in chapter 4.[30] In that examination, I observed that Revel's journal turns him from a detective of the external world to a detective of the internal one. Theodor Reik was one of the first to recognize the kinship between the detective and the analyst, comparing Freud's technique to that of Sherlock Holmes. However, Freud responded that he preferred to be compared to Giovanni Morelli, a nineteenth-century art scholar who specialized in detecting fakes.[31] The exposure of the guilty person and of the fake also lies at the heart of novels like *Passing Time*, *Homo Faber*, and *The Lie*. The plots of these literary works resemble the psychoanalytic session as conceived by Lacan in that they center upon a subject who writes his own life story and names his own desire.[32]

Most readers agree that Faber begins his narrative in an effort to prove that he did not know until too late that his lover, Sabeth, was his daughter (a variation of the Oedipal incest mytheme, as we saw in chapter 2 with Moravia's *The Lie*) and that he also cannot be blamed for her death. Butler, for example, accepts this position, but he also identifies a second purpose behind Faber's report—his need to "uphold his view of life as a system of unemotional orderliness in which all phenomena are satisfactorily accounted for."[33] However, in fulfilling this latter need, Faber exhibits, as Alan Latta points out, a "habit of dividing the phenomena of life into two groups and then attaching value judgments to them." On the one side—the side Faber approves and to which he subscribes—are probability, tech-

nology, rationality, and the male sex. On the other side—the side
that disgusts Faber and that he constantly attacks—are fate, nature,
irrationality, and the female sex.[34] But, as is the case when someone
protests too much, Faber is actually more on the side he attacks than
on that he defends; composing his story forces him to admit not only
that he is less innocent than he suspected but also that he is not the
man he thought he was.

Although critics have contended that Faber's self-exposure begins
midway in his report, when he describes his relationship with Sabeth, this is actually the point at which the contradictions become
so flagrant that even Faber, who has spent at least twenty years
building his self-image of a rational man, can no longer ignore them.
Sprinkled throughout his text are indications that his self-image is
really self-deception. For instance, it is not true, as Latta suggests,
that Faber uses metaphors only after he meets Sabeth.[35] To cite one
example, before the crash landing that causes him to spend several
days in the Mexican desert, Faber looks out the plane window and
sees

> swamps, shallow and turbid, divided by *tongues* of land, sand, the
> swamps were green in some places and in others red, the red of
> a lipstick, something I couldn't understand, they were really not
> swamps but lagoons, and where they reflected the sun they glit-
> tered *like tinsel or tinfoil*, anyhow with a metallic glint, then again
> they were sky-blue and watery (*like Ivy's eyes*) with yellow shoals
> and patches *like violet ink*, somber, probably due to underwater
> plants; at one point a river flowed into the swamp, brown *like
> milky American coffee*. (15, italics mine)

Considering its hesitations, this description is obviously not the work
of an experienced poet, but neither is it the objective report of a
scientist or of a man who a few pages later maintains that he cannot
see anything other than what he sees. Descriptive passages such as
this one, few though they are in the first half of Faber's narrative
(see also 42, 53, and 69), hint that Faber is not all he seems and thus
prepare us for the release of metaphor and the revealing of his true

character that Sabeth will draw out of him, and not just in their simile game.

Faber's propensity for metaphor is not the only quirk that shows him for what he is. To list a few of many other contradictions, Faber follows his nasty indictment of marriage (92–94) with his account of proposing to Sabeth (96). Later, during their trip through Italy, Faber attempts to respond to art as Sabeth has been doing all along but claims he is simply bored (113). Yet when he turns the corner in the museum and comes upon the *Head of a Sleeping Erinys*, he responds completely: "Here I found it—magnificent, impressive, superb, profoundly impressive. It was the stone head of a girl, so placed that when you leaned forward on your elbows you looked down upon it as though upon the face of a sleeping woman" (114). Next, Faber rationalizes that his stomach trouble is temporary, caused by stress or the environment, even though its frequent recurrences would urge a reasonable man to see a doctor. And, finally, there is Faber's surprise at the many sunsets appearing in the films he shot during his journeys through Mexico, America, Guatemala, and Italy: "three in the Tamaulipas desert alone, anyone would have thought I was traveling in sunsets" (196). The eye of the camera has seen past Faber's mask of sensibleness and captured his sentimental center.

But the contradiction that leads Faber to acknowledge these other inconsistencies is the most important one, the one that concerns his awareness of Sabeth's true relation to him *at the time* he began to think of seducing her. Faber denies that he had any idea that Sabeth was his daughter when he met her; after all, he did not even know he was a father. Yet other evidence suggests that Faber had more than just a suspicion of her actual paternity. For one thing, from the moment of their first meeting, Sabeth reminds him of Hanna, a woman he loved twenty years ago, his first and perhaps only real love. Faber disregards this physical proof by telling himself that "probably every young girl would somehow remind me of Hanna" (79). Significantly, Sabeth seems to resemble Faber too, since several persons, including his former professor, assume she is his daughter, but Faber never ponders the implications of these remarks nor does

98

he notice the resemblance himself. In fact, as their relationship becomes more intimate, Faber declares that Sabeth's likeness to Hanna strikes him less and less frequently (118). The more he wants Sabeth, the more he builds a wall of rationalizations to keep him from seeing the truth. When Faber learns that Hanna *is* Sabeth's mother, he accepts Sabeth's word that Joachim is her father, even though he knows that the last time he saw Hanna, approximately twenty-one years ago (Sabeth's age plus nine months), she was pregnant with his child. So much does Faber want to be convinced he is not Sabeth's father that he juggles the relevant dates "until the sum worked out the way I wanted it: She could only be Joachim's child!" (125).

Faber keeps the knowledge that Sabeth is his daughter from his consciousness even after Sabeth's accident and hospitalization. And yet this knowledge is just waiting to surface and be confirmed. In his first conversation with Hanna in twenty years, Faber agrees with her that he is not Sabeth's father. But while taking a bath, he starts

thinking about statistics, thinking about Joachim, who had hanged himself, thinking about the future, thinking until I shivered, until I didn't know what I was thinking, it was as though I couldn't make up my mind to recognize my own thoughts. . . .

What was the matter with me?

I didn't know myself. (140)

This last sentence is deliberately ambiguous. Faber characteristically refuses to acknowledge these emotional, illogical, macabre thoughts as belonging to him. But also, because of this "blindness of his seeing eye" (to borrow Freud's phrase), he, like Oedipus, does not know himself. As this self-knowledge comes closer to surfacing, Faber's imagination runs wild. The tub becomes an Etruscan sarcophagus, and Faber wishes not for death but never to have existed, a wish that Oedipus also expressed after discovering the truth about himself.[36] Faber reveals here that he *knows* the truth and has apparently known it for some time. However, as Lacan suggests, truth consists not in knowledge but in recognition, a point Faber finally reaches the next day when Hanna directly confronts him with the fact of his paternity.

"'You know,' [Hanna] said, 'that she is your child?'" "I knew," Faber writes (164).

In naming his relationship to Sabeth, Faber names his guilt; his self-incrimination, like Oedipus', derives from a failure to apprehend origins. Given all the clues that Faber has purposely overlooked, it is appropriate that he yearns finally for an Oedipal resolution. After Sabeth's death, Faber watches a film he had taken during their trip together, facing, for the first time, her death and his part in it. She no longer exists except on film—no substitute, he now realizes, for life—and Faber cannot help but assume that he has caused her death by being in her life. Sitting in the dining car of a train, Faber concludes, "All I wished was that I had never existed. . . . Why not take these two forks, hold them upright in my hands and let my head fall, so as to get rid of my eyes?" (203). Although Faber resists the temptation, he obviously thinks, as Oedipus' blinding suggests about himself, that his mistake has been in not *seeing* what was in front of him all along.

In writing his story, Faber writes the truth about his past and himself. Although he cannot completely shed the patterns by which he has lived for at least twenty years, he reconciles to a great degree the duality within himself. While in Caracas, where he composes the report of his time with Sabeth, Faber surrenders to the romantic, emotional side of life that he previously scorned and refused to admit he shared in. His relationship with Sabeth, as well as the experience of writing about it, decenters Faber; he begins to take a genuine interest in other people. Just how far he has come can be seen in two reversals. First, having once denied that he could hear eternity, Faber now spends an afternoon that "looked absolutely like eternity, blue, unbearable, but beautiful, but endless" (187), and he even defines it: "The main thing is to stand up to the light, to joy (like our child) in the knowledge that I shall be extinguished in the light over gorse, asphalt, and sea, to stand up to time, or rather to eternity in the instant. To be eternal means to have existed" (210). Second, and finally, in our last view of Faber, we find a man who now possesses such delicate inner sight that he knows, even before the doctors who will cut him open to examine his stomach, that nothing can be done to save him. Such unrelenting self-knowledge reminds one of the divinely sighted Oedipus who leads Theseus to the site of his (Oedipus') own grave.

Moravia's *The Lie*: Man the Unmasker

The preceding analysis of *Homo Faber* recalls the discussion in chapter 2 of Moravia's *The Lie*. In fact, Francesco's interpretation of Oedipus, which he applies to his own situation, also seems an apt summary of Faber's case. Francesco claims that during his years as King of Thebes, Oedipus "has not been so much ignorant as unwilling" to know that Jocasta is his mother and that he killed his father. Oedipus is blind, Francesco asserts, because he loves Jocasta, wants power, and most of all, fears knowing the truth. When he finally opens his eyes (paradoxically by blinding himself), Oedipus passes from noninvolvement to involvement and sees the truth about his past and himself: "He sees, in short, that his crime consisted not so much in succumbing to certain passions as in deluding himself into thinking he did not feel them and in making use of this delusion to give vent to them with impunity" (80–82).

Francesco's story is like Faber's (and Haze's and Oedipus') in that each man progresses from noninvolvement and self-ignorance to involvement and self-awareness. An aspiring novelist, Francesco claims he begins his diary because he believes that the routine details of everyday life will provide the material for a novel of the genuine, as opposed to the action-based novel of artificiality (33). Ironically, the very day Francesco implements this plan, his life changes from the routine to the action filled, but *only because* he simultaneously decides to investigate a letter received ten years ago telling him that his wife was a procuress. Francesco is either lying about his purpose for writing or the act of composition forces him, as it does Faber, to stop living a lie.

Also like Faber, Francesco discovers the truth about himself in the lies that appear spontaneously—and without his immediate awareness—in the pages of his journal. As he concludes:

In reality, the diary is always sincere, always truthful; it is merely a question of seeking out the sincerity and truth behind the events.

This is the reason why diaries, journals, autobiographies, confessions, and memoirs are all more or less untruthful in a factual sense and truthful in a psychological sense. They are like a mirror in which anyone who looks at himself cannot help assuming an attitude, in some way or other. The truth lies not so much in the image as in the character of the person who, at the very moment in which the mirror reflects his image, creates himself, so to speak, as though by enchantment. But this personage cannot be accepted just as he is; he must be interpreted, submitted to a critical examination. It will then become apparent that he is the result of almost automatic lies and reticences and travesties. (309–10)

In this description of diaries, journals, autobiographies, confessions, and memoirs, Francesco does not clarify *who* is "seeking out the sincerity and truth behind the events" or who is doing the interpreting, submitting the "personage" to critical examination. In many autobiographical fictional narratives—for instance, Walker Percy's *Lancelot*—the seeker is the reader, who sees through or beyond the narrator to the truth. And while readers certainly respond this way to *The Lie* and *Homo Faber*, in both stories the narrator himself also participates in this discovery. To some extent, any story that traces a protagonist's movement from *méconnaissance* to *reconnaissance* will resemble *Oedipus the King*; however, the novels explored in this chapter intensify the resemblance by employing various Oedipal mythemes—particularly and always, the self-incrimination mytheme that implies self-discovery.

Ironically, these Oedipal self-disclosure stories do not solve the problem of the unreliable narrator, for what such works ultimately demonstrate is that searching for the truth about one's self is an unending process. In his description of personal narratives, Francesco says, "The truth lies not so much in the image as in the character of the person who, *at the very moment* in which the mirror reflects his image, creates himself, so to speak, as though by enchantment." I emphasize the phrase "at the very moment" because it suggests that self-discovery is a process, not a product, which depends upon the questions being asked and where the seeker stands at the time of the questioning. Lacan identifies the narrative extension of Oedipus' story into *Oedipus at Colonus* with "the radical impossibility of ever burying the speech of the unconscious."[37] Felman explains, "The end of Oedipus analysis, in other words, is the discovery that analysis, and in particular didactic self-analysis, is in effect interminable."[38] Just so, the Oedipal self-disclosure story is finally about the discovery of self-delusion. This may make the narrators of these stories more honest and more tormented, but it does not make them more reliable.

The Oedipal Self-Disclosure Story

The disposition of the Oedipal mythemes in *Wise Blood*, *Homo Faber*, and *The Lie* forces us not only to reexamine the Oedipus myth itself but also to reassess the priority that the twentieth century has given to Freud's reading of it.[39] Admittedly, these novels all employ the incest mytheme and therefore continue to acknowledge the power of desire within a familial context. Such acknowledgment seems inevitable—at least until the structure of the family in the Western world changes. As André Green observes, "To say that the Oedipus complex is universal is to say that every human being is born of two progenitors, one of a sex identical to his [or her] own, the other of a different sex."[40] Until this biological reality changes, we can constitute a person's experience in many ways, but we will still have to account for the effect of the infant-mother-father relationship on the psyche.

But despite the presence of the family romance in all these novels,[41] each seems more interested in the way the mind defends itself against naming that which we desire. Certainly, Freud did not underestimate the importance of defense mechanisms, since his theory of the Oedipus complex is based on the child's repression of those desires that he or she is forbidden to act on. However, like some contemporary analysts, O'Connor, Frisch, and Moravia depart from Freud's reading of the Oedipus myth by refusing to privilege the child's attraction to a parent. For these writers, the power of a desire to overwhelm and control an individual takes precedence over the origin of the desire. In fact, the use of the self-blinding mytheme by O'Connor, Frisch, and Moravia helps to support the view that contemporary society has moved away from Freud's reading of the myth as a paradigm for childhood development. Instead of presenting blindness as punishment for incest (the psychoanalytic idea of symbolic castration), these three writers use it to confirm the Sophoclean point that the blind man can see more clearly than the man with perfect vision. For them, as for Sophocles, lack of sight represents insight;[42] Oedipus' crucial crime was failing to see what was right before his eyes.

According to Alister Cameron, when speaking about the action of *Oedipus the King*, we are better advised to refer to "the Oedipus question" rather than to "the Oedipus complex": "For it is a question, not a complex, which comprehends the whole and to which everything responds. 'Who am I?' in a very real sense *is* the action" (50). The dramatic enactment of this question describes equally well the plots of *Wise Blood, Homo Faber,* and *The Lie.* Rereading Freud has brought us back to Sophocles.

C H A P T E R 6

The Epistemology of the Oedipus Myth

■

It would be tempting to try to discover the rule by which certain myths may seem to exercise a greater spell than others, but to say so would be to say it in terms of ourselves, to confess that it is some conflict within our own civilization that has given to the Oedipus story some pre-eminent claim on our imagination. A psychology of myth-makers would be required to describe the relationship of inner need and chosen form.

—WILLIAM RIGHTER[1]

In fact, from the time of its first performance some twenty-four hundred years ago in the theatre of Dionysus at Athens, I doubt if [*Oedipus the King*] has ever been seen so much as it has been during the last twenty-five years. Why? Certainly this interest must have something to do with our particular state of mind.

—ALISTER CAMERON[2]

If it is true, as William Doty proposes, that "a culture is the mythic stories it tells,"[3] then certainly the evidence of the three preceding chapters should persuade even the most stubborn skeptic that the Oedipus myth has gained and continues to hold a prominent place in the twentieth-century imagination. These chapters have shown that this myth has been used not only frequently and cogently but also widely in modern fiction, ranging from stories that drift far from the mainstream, such as Philip José Farmer's "Riders of the Purple Wage," to those that live within it, such as Max Frisch's *Homo Faber*. The appeal of the Oedipus myth has been strong enough to inspire some very good writers—Wells, O'Connor, Pynchon, Robbe-

Grillet, Frisch, Moravia, and Butor—to work with it. In fact, as we saw in chapter 2, William Faulkner can also be included in this group; and his case provides compelling testimony of this myth's power, since, according to his own admission, Faulkner retold Oedipus' story in *Light in August* without immediately realizing he was doing so.

But as William Righter implies in the passage quoted above, pinning down the reason why the Oedipus myth has grabbed our imagination is a much more difficult task than convincing the skeptical that such a hold exists. Many theories about the myth's meaning have been advanced in this century, the most famous belonging to Freud, who claims that Oedipus' fate moves us because it might have been our own, because we have secretly wished to murder our father and marry our mother (or vice versa). However, numerous speculations have succeeded Freud's, and they reveal the capacity of the myth to speak to a changing world. To mention just one of these recently expressed ideas, Alister Cameron proposes that the continuing power of *Oedipus the King* can be traced to its tragic view. He claims that since 1945, when the world became generally aware of the possibility and potential of nuclear war, the public situation towards life and death

> has come to bear a distinct resemblance to what the Greeks learned to call "tragic"—that is, a situation in which the possibility that we cannot escape our fate is all too clear. Perhaps then we too, like the Greek, feel the need of looking at the possibility squarely, and perhaps even feel, however obscurely, that we may see or learn something there which will help us to take a hand in our fate, something which our own theater has not been able to provide. (xix)[4]

Certainly it would be shortsighted to suggest that a study covering selected appearances of the Oedipus myth could produce a theory that would supersede Freud's or Cameron's—or any other hypothesis. Indeed, displacement is not the goal. As I argued in chapter 1, the "mythicity" of a myth lies in its ability to make us feel that it expresses the inexpressible. Our perpetual need to retell and interpret the Oedipus myth must therefore be seen as an indication of its potency, of its ability to continue to speak to us of unnamed desires that elude our consciousness. The question, then, is not whether another theory can be proposed but how a study of restricted scope can produce such a proposal. My high expectations for this limited survey derive from the principal assumption behind it: that myth functions like a language when used in fiction.

Ferdinand de Saussure's famous distinction between *langue* (language) and *parole* (speech) suggests that language must be analyzed as a formal system and as a finished or an occurring action. The first enterprise belongs essentially to the realm of language theory; the second to that of language performance. This study engages in both of these enterprises. Chapter 1, which devises a means for identifying the signs of myth, and chapter 2, which describes how these signs acquire meaning, attempt to establish myth within a fictional context as a language system. To put this in linguistics terms, these chapters concentrate on questions of syntactics and semantics. But in discussing how readers respond to specific appearances of a myth's signs (its mythemes), chapter 2 also investigates the communicative activity triggered by myth. Here we turn to questions of pragmatics, that is, to how a language's signs are used by encoders and decoders. This direction is continued in the next three chapters, which look specifically at how a number of twentieth-century writers have employed the mythemes of the Oedipus myth and how readers (primarily a single reader, myself as critic) have interpreted them.[5]

In short, this study deals with the Oedipus myth as a potential and a real language, selected and actualized by various encoders and decoders. In effect, it gathers together the speech acts of a specific speech community. Linguists have always implicitly recognized that language is a mirror reflecting the attitudes and concerns of its users, but only within the last thirty years have they methodically developed this idea. Psycholinguistics, sociolinguistics, socio-psycholinguistics, and ethnolinguistics are all relatively young disciplines committed to analyzing problems involving the relation of the individual and society to language. Scholars of these fields have shown that individuals, without consciously knowing it, reveal their biases and preoccupations in the signs they use and in their interpretations of these signs. More important to our purposes, these researchers have also demonstrated that entire speech communities reveal themselves in the same way. These practices and findings suggest that we, too, might reach a better understanding of our relation to the Oedipus myth and of its relation to us by examining how various members of our speech community (specific fiction writers) use this "language."

We can pursue this understanding from several directions, but two courses hold the most promise. First, we can analyze the speech process itself, focusing on the choice and distribution of mythemes, much as a sociolinguist would examine the word choices and syntax of a society in order to acquire knowledge of its mind-set, predilections, and habits. Second, we can look for a pattern to the changes made in the contents of various mythemes. We have identified such changes in the separate discussions of the three genres using the Oedipus myth, but by bringing together those results, we could uncover a larger pattern revealing at least one aspect of the Oedipus myth that makes it so accommodating to the concerns of our age— and so fascinating to us.

An important precaution must accompany these endeavors.[6] As noted in chapter 2, mythemic changes, selection, and distribution can reflect the predispositions of a particular work's characters or author. Looking for universals and refusing to generalize from isolated cases will prevent us from mistaking textual or authorial exigencies for societal ones. For example, as we saw in chapters 2 and 5, both Moravia and Frisch transform the principals of the incest mytheme from mother and son to father and daughter/stepdaughter. While it is tempting to propose that this substitution shows that Western patriarchal society engages more frequently in one kind of incest than another—and research would support this conclusion[7]— it is just as likely that the modification arises from the demands of the text. Both *The Lie* and *Homo Faber* center upon a middle-aged man in the middle of a mid-life crisis, and the desire for a younger woman, even young enough to be a daughter, is often part of this experience. Without the supporting sociological studies (which happen to be available in this case), we would have to view this mythemic change as an interesting coincidence, not a significant trend.

The information we seek lies, then, in more widespread—and perhaps more subtle—changes than those made by two authors. Keeping this in mind, let us review the preceding three chapters to determine which Oedipal mythemes have been most consistently used in the twentieth-century fiction we have examined and how their contents have been altered. These findings can then be analyzed for larger patterns that might point toward one reason for the Oedipus myth's strong claim on the imagination of the modern Western world.

As we have seen, several modern science fiction authors have infused the Sphinx mytheme (8) with impotence by enfeebling both the Sphinx and her Oedipal opponent. Instead of a contest between intellectual equals as in the Oedipus myth, dystopian stories such as *The Time Machine, Venus on the Half-Shell,* "Riders of the Purple Wage," and *Deus Irae* give us mute or inept Sphinxes—representing the loss of wisdom in a future world—and incompetent, unsuccessful, or untested saviors—suggesting a respective loss of ingenuity. No single riddle or answer holds the key to salvation for these future worlds. On the contrary, riddles keep popping up everywhere, unsolved and insolvable.

In the antidetective fiction we have treated, the investigation into a mystery (mytheme 13) resolves itself, as it does in the Oedipus myth, with the detective discovering that he or she is the guilty party (mytheme 15). *The Erasers, Passing Time,* and *The Crying of Lot 49* stress the detective's ineptitude and helplessness both during and after the inquiry. The blundering of these detectives can be traced to Oedipus, who from one perspective seems not so much to uncover the truth as to stumble upon it; but Robbe-Grillet, Butor, and Pynchon accent this feature to such a degree that it dominates the other components of these two Oedipal mythemes. Furthermore, the detectives of these contemporary novels fail to find any release from the discovery of their own complicity and the disordering of their view of reality, as Oedipus achieves in his self-blinding. Their investigation of a mystery turns, like Oedipus', into an investigation of reality; however, the final mystery is reality itself—a mystery these detectives are incapable of solving.

The investigatory (13) and self-incrimination (15) mythemes found in antidetective fiction also appear in a number of contemporary psychological narratives, along with the self-blinding mytheme (17). As is true of Oedipus and his postmodern detective counterparts, the self-knowledge attained by the protagonists of *Wise Blood*, *Homo Faber*, and *The Lie* centers upon the realization that they misunderstand themselves and reality. Significantly, Haze Motes is the only one of these protagonists to objectify his lack of insight with the act of self-blinding. Within the Christian context of O'Connor's world, such an act has meaning as an acceptance of divine omnipotence and final truth. However, for characters like Walter Faber, whose discovery of self-delusion means a loss of absolutes, blindness is the condition of life; self-blinding would be superfluous. Simply put, in a novel like *Homo Faber*, self-delusion is recursive, and believing that a final truth exists would be the ultimate self-delusion.

In sum, the Oedipal mythemes used most prominently and frequently in the twentieth-century fiction we have explored (excluding the incest and patricide mythemes that form the basis for the family romance) are the encounter with the Sphinx (8); the investigation into a mystery (13); the self-incrimination or self-recognition (15); and the self-blinding (17). Taken together, these last three mythemes make up the central action of *Oedipus the King*, and so one's first impulse is to explain their appearance in twentieth-century stories as a wholesale borrowing of the plot that Aristotle named the most tightly constructed in all of Greek tragedy. But this explanation does not account for the use of the Sphinx mytheme nor does it hint at a reason for the Oedipus myth's appeal beyond the desire for compact action. However, these three mythemes are also related thematically in that they treat the subject of knowledge, a relationship that not only connects them to the Sphinx mytheme but also seems a more promising source for assessing the myth's appeal.

That knowledge is a principal theme of the Oedipus myth goes without saying,[8] but these four mythemes remind us that we are often too simplistic in our understanding of this theme. Each of these

110

Oedipal signs seems to concentrate on a different kind of knowledge. The investigation into a mystery involves knowledge of "the Other"; the self-incrimination implies knowledge about the self; the meeting with the Sphinx has to do with knowledge of the world; and the self-blinding, although associated with self-insight, also concerns knowledge of that which exists beyond one's immediate world—in some cases, knowledge of the supernatural.

Oedipus' history reveals that human experience must embrace all four types of knowledge; for although his fame rests upon his knowledge of the world (his answering of the Sphinx' riddle), his infamy results from his lack of knowledge about the Other, the self, and the gods. Had he known who he was, he would not have committed incest or patricide; had he deciphered Apollo's oracle correctly, he would not have become the guilty defendant of his own prosecution. Bernard Knox observes that Oedipus' discovery of his ignorance turns him into "the paradigm, the example, the object lesson. 'I have your destiny as an example,' sings the chorus, 'and call no man happy.'"[9] If this is true, then Oedipus' story stands as a warning not against the specific transgressions of incest and patricide but against the general error of elevating one kind of knowledge over the others.

But having determined that the fiction we have studied has given a prominent place and emphasis to the four Oedipal mythemes dealing most centrally with the acquisition of knowledge, how do we explain the fact that within this fiction these four signs transmit the opposite message: human beings cannot know anything for certain? Is this an irreconcilable inconsistency, or does it reveal the universal mythemic change we seek? The answer to this question seems to be a little of both.

In chapter 4, I argued that *Oedipus the King* is more an antidetective than a detective story, because the knowledge that Oedipus attains is not only an absolute and horrible truth about himself but also the contradictory knowledge that absolute truths do not exist, or at least cannot be known by humans. The gods may be omniscient, yet this gives little intellectual comfort to mortals, who glimpse this divine knowledge only by correctly reading the prophecies of the mantic oracle, an act that, as Oedipus' example emphasizes, is as likely to disclose the limits of human knowledge as the truth. This interpretation of Oedipus' history is supported by Knox, who claims that Oedipus learns what Socrates recognized, that the truly wise man is the one who knows he is not wise,[10] and by Dodds, who views Oedipus as "a kind of symbol of the human intelligence which cannot rest until it has solved all the riddles—even the last riddle, to which the answer is that human happiness is built on an illusion."[11]

As Dodds admits, this interpretation is more inferred than stated in Sophocles' plays, but it does not, I believe, controvert the integrity or the events of the myth. In fact, to requote some lines cited in chapter 4, Oedipus, near the end of his life, tells Theseus that "you cannot fail of your reward / In giving Oedipus this dwelling-place, / Unless heaven means to play him false again" (*Oedipus at Colonus* 90). Such a statement seems to indicate that Oedipus has become acutely aware of the uncertain nature of human knowledge. In using the Oedipus myth to express the inability to know absolutely, many modern authors have thus developed a theme that is primarily implicit in the myth. Rather than see this trend as a modifying of any particular mytheme, we should probably describe it as an intensifying of the contents of several mythemes. Nevertheless, this widespread accentuation not only provides a different angle on Oedipus' story, it also suggests a source of the myth's fascination for the twentieth century. We have been drawn to the Oedipus myth again and again because it speaks of knowledge or, more accurately, of the limits of knowledge.

Frank McConnell observes that the twentieth century has inherited and nurtured a longstanding tradition that claims that the human mind and the structure of outer events are, in some way, supremely connected and that science can discover the nature of this link.[12] In fact, we can trace this tradition back at least to Sophocles' time with its Protagorean belief that man is the measure of all things and that man can measure all things. But, McConnell continues, the theories of scientists like Werner Heisenberg and Thomas Kuhn and of mathematicians like Kurt Gödel have helped to replace this tradition with "a new 'scientifically sanctioned' view of man, a view that regards him as isolated from the universe around him not only by virtue of his intelligence, but by virtue of the *limits* of that intelligence."[13] As Bertrand Russell puts it, the only doctrine that has proved infallible is the one declaring that all human knowledge is uncertain, inexact, and partial.[14] Moreover, the field of psychoanalysis has also confirmed our inability to know absolutely by inferring the existence of the unconscious. According to Jacques Lacan, "Analysis appears on the scene to announce that there is knowledge that does not know itself, knowledge that is supported by the signifier as such."[15]

Oedipus' history, as various modern authors have shown, encompasses both traditions, the old and the new. Michael J. O'Brien notes that before his fall, Oedipus stands as a proponent of the idea that "man's knowledge, especially his technological and scientific knowledge, constituted his chief protection against disaster and his chief claim to greatness,"[16] a position Oedipus apparently earned by answering the Sphinx' riddle, by possessing knowledge of how the world works. That we still want to believe the universe operates meaningfully—and that we will discover how—can be seen in the actions of characters such as Oedipa Maas, Wallas, Jacques Revel, Simon Wagstaff, and Walter Faber. That we must learn not to expect final meaning is the point of their stories and, as twentieth-century writers would have it, a salient point of Oedipus'.

Ultimately, of course, Oedipus' story is not identical to those of his modern counterparts. The gods are, after all, present and indirectly active in both *Oedipus the King* and *Oedipus at Colonus*. Their intermediaries, the oracle and Tiresias, are also available to turn vague suspicions into meaningful truths, even though such truths may become blindingly obvious only in retrospect. Yet most twentieth-century narratives using the Oedipus myth lack these assurances and reassurances. There are no prophecies, no visionaries, no *deus ex machinas*. The only real exceptions to this rule are O'Connor's *Wise Blood*, Dick and Zelazny's *Deus Irae*, and Verne's *An Antarctic Mystery*, with their Christian frameworks and their faith in an all-seeing power. The typical contemporary Oedipus must grope in the dark toward a dim light that turns out to be only another sign pointing to another dim light, ad infinitum.

To emphasize the limits of human knowledge, twentieth-century writers employing the Oedipus myth, especially those employing it since 1945, have also duplicated the Oedipal experience in the reading experience. David Grossvogel identifies the main exercise of the Oedipus text as hermeneutical: "Both Oedipus and the reader [and here we can add most of the characters we have studied] are given a text to decipher."[17] However, readers who believe that this will be an easy task soon find such an expectation destroyed. Red herrings, ambiguous or double endings, unreliable narrators, and missing information eventually lead us to the same conclusion reached by the Oedipal figures of these texts: there are no final answers. Further, just as self-blinding does not end Oedipus' attempt to interpret his "text," so reading the final page of the Oedipal work does not conclude our similar effort. In his exile from Thebes, Oedipus again takes up the role of questioner,[18] seeking especially to comprehend the text of his past. "Was I the sinner?" he asks the elders of Colonus, "Repaying wrong for wrong—that was no sin, / Even were it wittingly done, as it was not. / I did not know the way I went" (*Oedipus at Colonus* 79). Similarly, we emerge from a typical Oedipal text with questions. Like Oedipus, we return to the text, probing it for additional clues and revising our initial interpretation, yet fully aware that our understanding can change but will never be complete. Of course, this type of participatory story with its ultimate nonsolution characterizes a great deal of contemporary fiction, but nowhere, I think, is the point so clearly made as in the Oedipal narrative, where our experience mirrors the character's experience, which mirrors Oedipus' experience.

Finally, it is worth stressing again that the entire reason for the Western world's attraction to the Oedipus myth in the twentieth century cannot derive only from its ability to accommodate the epistemological movement of our era from positivism to relativity and indeterminacy. The infinite power of the Oedipus myth to engage and enthrall is perhaps best summarized by René Girard:

As I try to manipulate my Oedipus metaphor and as it manipulates me, I realize how inadequate I am to the task of suggesting the infinite perspective which it opens to us. Far from undermining the relevance of the myth—and of Greek tragedy, as Freud himself, with all his genius, still unfortunately did—by calling it a dream (and Freud saw infinitely more in Oedipus than all Rationalists combined, beginning with Aristotle), the present orientation of research confirms the power of myth and the relevance of early Greek thought to our own experience. We can begin to unveil in the myth more than a coherent structure, a real matrix of diachronically ordered structures whose suggestiveness as metaphors of our individual and collective predicament—or should I say as *structural models?*—appears almost unlimited.[19]

Oedipus continues to fascinate us because he continues to speak to—and for—us. In retelling and interpreting his story, we hear him say different things; the analysis in which we have placed him seems interminable.

Notes
Works Cited
Index

Notes

■

Introduction: Reading Myth from Joyce to Pynchon

1. John Vickery, *Myths and Texts: Strategies of Incorporation and Displacement* (Baton Rouge: Louisiana State UP, 1983) 1.

2. John Vickery, "Orpheus and Persephone: Uses and Meanings," *Classical Mythology in Twentieth-Century Thought and Literature*, ed. Wendell M. Aycock and Theodore M. Klein (Lubbock: Texas Tech P, 1980) 188.

3. Vickery, *Myths and Texts* 1–2.

4. John White, in his *Mythology in the Modern Novel: A Study of Prefigurative Techniques* (Princeton: Princeton UP, 1971); and in his "Mythological Fiction and the Reading Process," *Literary Criticism and Myth*, ed. Joseph P. Strelka (University Park: Penn State UP, 1980) 72–92.

5. White mentions in particular Iser's study of Joyce's *Ulysses*, which suggests that the myth gives the reader "signals" that create expectations ("Der Archetyp als Leerform. Erzählschablonen und Kommunikation in Joyces *Ulysses*," *Terror und Spiel. Probleme der Mythenrezeption*, ed. Manfred Fuhrmann, *Poetik und Hermeneutik* 4 [Munich: Fink Verlag, 1971] 369–408; trans. and rpt. as "Patterns of Communication in Joyce's *Ulysses*," in Iser's *The Implied Reader: Patterns of Communication in Prose Fiction From Bunyan to Beckett* [Baltimore: Johns Hopkins UP, 1974] 196–233). As White points out, Iser is concerned here with the stylistic repercussions of the *Odyssey* prefiguration in the individual chapters of Joyce's novel. But in suggesting that such a mythological background offers "an interpretive *possibility*, Iser shows one way in which the reading process can be treated" ("Mythological Fiction" 83).

6. Stanley Fish, headnote, "What Is Stylistics and Why Are They Saying Such Terrible Things about It?," *Is There a Text in This Class? The Authority of Interpretive Communities* (Cambridge: Harvard UP, 1980) 68. Consider also Leonard Orr's observation that both Wittgenstein and Heidegger demonstrated, at great length, that "the rules one sets predetermine not only one's actions, the course of the interpretive investigation, but, in fact,

the results of that investigation" ("From Procrustean Criticism to Process Hermeneutics," *Sub-stance* 25 [1980]: 75).

7. Besides various kinds of criticism—from Barthes' *S/Z* to White's studies of mythology and criticism—my views in this book have been formulated—and confirmed—by the reading experiences of students in two comparative studies classes I taught at The Ohio State University in the winters of 1988 and 1989. Although the focus in each of these classes was slightly different, they both centered upon the Oedipus myth in twentieth-century fiction and the process of reading fiction using myth.

8. Robert Scholes, *Structuralism in Literature* (New Haven: Yale UP, 1974) 40. Some reader-response critics are, in fact, skeptical of any text-based paradigm, arguing that structures are in the reader, not the text. See especially the work of David Bleich, *Readers and Feelings: An Introduction to Subjective Criticism* (Urbana: NCTE, 1975); and *Subjective Criticism* (Baltimore: Johns Hopkins UP, 1978).

9. Northrop Frye, "Literature and Myth," *Relations of Literary Study*, ed. James Thorpe (New York: MLA, 1967) 38.

10. George Steiner, *Antigones: How the Antigone Legend Has Endured in Western Literature, Art, and Thought* (Oxford: Clarendon, 1986) 6.

11. Peter Rudnytsky, *Freud and Oedipus* (New York: Columbia UP, 1987) 96–97.

12. For studies of such fiction, see Bernard De Voto, "Freud's Influence on Literature," *Saturday Review of Literature* 20 (1939): 10–11; parts of Frederick J. Hoffman's *Freudianism and the Literary Mind*, 2nd ed. (Baton Rouge: Louisiana State UP, 1957); and Francesco Aristide Ancona, *Writing the Absence of the Father: Undoing Oedipal Structures in the Contemporary American Novel* (Lanham, MD: UP of America, 1986).

13. To mention just one of many, Vladimir Propp suggests that we are attracted to Oedipus because his suffering is personal—unusual for a Greek hero—and he thus attains an individuality that makes him truly human: in Oedipus, "man enters European history" ("Oedipus in the Light of Folklore," trans. Polly Coote, *Oedipus: A Folklore Casebook*, ed. Lowell Edmunds and Alan Dundes [New York: Garland, 1983] 118). Most of the proposals come, like Propp's, from a specific perspective (e.g., Propp speaks from the position of a folklorist). As we will see, studying fictional uses of Oedipus' story demands that we enlarge our perspective and see things from multiple viewpoints; therefore, our understanding should be more comprehensive, although that does not mean it will necessarily be conclusive or more "correct."

14. Twentieth-century uses of figures such as Pan, Prometheus, Orpheus, Heracles, and Ulysses have been examined in one or more book-length studies, as have the adaptations of similar heroes such as Jesus, Don Juan,

Faust, Frankenstein, and those found in the Arthurian legend. See Patricia Merivale, *Pan the Goat-God: His Myth in Modern Times* (Cambridge: Harvard UP, 1969); Walter A. Strauss, *Descent and Return: The Orphic Theme in Modern Literature* (Cambridge: Harvard UP, 1971); Eva Kushner, *Le mythe d'Orphée dans la littérature française contemporaine* (Paris: Nizet, 1961); Raymond Trousson, *Le thème de Prométhée dans la littérature européene*, 2 vols. (Geneva: Librairie Droz, 1964); L. Awad, *The Theme of Prometheus in English and French Literature: A Study of Literary Influence* (Cairo: n.p., 1963); G. K. Galinsky, *The Heracles Theme* (Oxford: Oxford UP, 1972); W. B. Stanford, *The Ulysses Theme: A Study in the Adaptability of a Traditional Hero*, 2nd ed. (Ann Arbor: U of Michigan P, 1968); Theodore Ziolkowski, *Fictional Transfigurations of Jesus* (Princeton: Princeton UP, 1972); Leo Weinstein, *The Metamorphosis of Don Juan* (Stanford: Stanford UP, 1959); M. I. Sicard, *Don Juan: mythe et réalité* (Toulouse: Plon, 1967); Chris Baldick, ed., *In Frankenstein's Shadow: Myth, Monstrosity, and Nineteenth-Century Writing* (Oxford: Oxford UP, 1986); André Dabezies, *Visages de Faust au XXe siècle: littérature, idéologie, et mythe* (Paris: Presses Universitaires de France, 1967); J. M. Smeed, *Faust in Literature* (London: Oxford UP, 1975); Raymond Thompson, *The Return from Avalon: A Study of the Arthurian Legend in Modern Fiction* (Westport: Greenwood, 1985). Of course, some of these studies deal only in part with twentieth-century fiction.

Two ambitious and useful dissertations have been written on Oedipus' literary representations—Richard Fabrizio, "The Complex Oedipus: The Oedipus Figure in European Literature," diss., New York U, 1967; and Andrew Steele Horton, Jr., "The Oedipus Tyrannus Theme in Western Literature," diss., U of Illinois at Champaign-Urbana, 1973—but no one has yet concentrated solely on the Oedipus myth's subsistence in the fiction of this century.

15. Patrick Mullahy, *Oedipus Myth and Complex: A Review of Psychoanalytic Theory* (1948; New York: Grove, 1955) 90.

1. Myths and Their Signs

1. William Righter, *Myth and Literature* (London: Routledge, 1975) 7.

2. Vickery, *Myths and Texts* 2.

3. G. S. Kirk, *The Nature of Greek Myths* (1974; New York: Penguin, 1976) 27–28.

4. Harry Slochower, *Mythopoesis: Mythic Patterns in the Literary Classics* (Detroit: Wayne State UP, 1970) 40.

5. Kirk 18.

6. Consider William G. Doty's observation: "'Myth,' 'mythic,' 'mythical,' and 'mythological' have been utilized very much as the individual critic has desired, and often nonreflectively" (*Mythography: The Study of Myths and Rituals* [Tuscaloosa: U of Alabama P, 1986] 174).

7. Eric Gould, *Mythical Intentions in Modern Literature* (Princeton: Princeton UP, 1981) 11. Subsequent page references to this work are cited parenthetically within the text.

8. Marcel Detienne, *The Creation of Mythology*, trans. Margaret Cook (Chicago: U of Chicago P, 1986) 1.

9. Roland Barthes, "Myth Today," *Mythologies*, trans. Annette Lavers (New York: Hill, 1972) 110.

10. For a more complete survey and description of this interpretive tradition, see Raphael Patai's "Myth Interpretation Through the Ages," chap. 1, *Myth and Modern Man* (Englewood Cliffs, NJ: Prentice, 1972) 10–46; and Doty's *Mythography*.

An apparent problem with this approach to myth is that it fails to clearly differentiate myths from similar narratives, such as folktales, fairy tales, legends, and parables, many of which are also retold and sponsor their own bodies of analysis. In fact, it seems to me that many, although not all, of these tales possess the characteristic of mythicity as I have defined it and that this power might explain why we hear people refer to the Faust myth, the Cinderella myth, and the Trickster myth, when folktale, fairy tale, or legend might be the more technically proper name. In the final analysis, the main difference between many of these narratives and myth is the kind of story they tell—a difference that is not all that meaningful to a poetics of the sort proposed here. The discussion that follows will thus be inclusive (it will pertain to all myths) but not necessarily exclusive (it will also pertain to some other tales).

Another concern with my approach to myth might be that it does not distinguish myths from archetypes. This concern seems especially important given that Gould, whose ideas about myth I borrow so heavily from, builds much of his case upon the archetype. Gould transforms Jung's understanding of the archetype—which is still the understanding that most readers have of this concept—into "a representation of experience resulting itself from the quite distinct intent to make an interpretation of the world" (33). Hence, for Gould, the archetype is at the heart of mythicity and is not, as with Jung, an essentialized symbolic product of a mysterious collective mind. As the core sign of myth that provides an externalized mode of expression for the interior meanings we find in our lives (Doty 188), Gould's archetype seems a useful shorthand for describing the unconscious desire that the myth is the conscious expression of. However, I avoid it here for several reasons. One, to do justice to Gould's conception of the archetype would require a lengthy discussion of Jung and Northrop Frye as well as of Gould. More important, for purposes I will detail later in this chapter, I have chosen to refer to the core sign of myth as the *mytheme,* and I do not want readers to confuse this term with the archetype. Within Gould's system, the archetype is a function of the open-endedness of discourse, a "transactional model" (125). In contrast, the mytheme as I define it is a specific action within a myth that is itself interpretable. The mytheme is thus a function of the myth, and its meaning will depend, in part, upon its interrelations with other mythemes within the myth. It does not lie behind the myth but is part and parcel of it.

11. Steiner 206.

12. Michel Foucault's observations on commentary are pertinent here. As he states,

> [Commentary] permits us to create new discourses ad infinitum: the top-heaviness of the original text, its permanence, its status as discourse ever capable of being brought up to date, the multiple or hidden meanings with which it is credited, the reticence and wealth it is believed to contain, all this creates an open possibility for discussion. On the other hand, whatever the techniques employed, commentary's only role is to say *finally,* what has silently been articulated *deep down.* It must—and the paradox is ever-changing yet inescapable—say, for the first time, what has already been said, and repeat tirelessly what was, nevertheless, never said. (*The Discourse on Language,* trans. Rupert Swyer, *The Archaelogy of Knowledge and The Discourse on Language* [New York: Pantheon, 1972] 221)

13. Reuben A. Brower, "Visual and Verbal Translation of Myth: Neptune in Virgil, Rubens, Dryden," *Myth, Symbol, and Culture,* ed. Clifford Geertz (New York: Norton, 1971) 155.

14. Alister Cameron, *The Identity of Oedipus the King* (New York: New York UP, 1968) vii. Subsequent page references to this work are cited parenthetically within the text.

15. John Parry, *The Psychology of Human Communication* (New York: American Elsevier, 1968) 45–46. Compare also Ferdinand de Saussure's idea that "a word can always evoke everything that can be associated with it in one way or another" (*Course in General Linguistics,* ed. Charles Bally and Albert Sechehaye, trans. Wade Baskin [New York: Philosophical Library, 1959] 126). I am also aware of the complicated history of the concepts of denotation and connotation; as Rosalind Coward and John Ellis observe, "The fixed relation of signifier and signified which is the object of linguistics is shown as only one moment of a process. It becomes fixed when the

conscious subject is constructed in a certain position in relation to the signifying chain" (*Language and Materialism: Developments in Semiology and the Theory of Signs* [London: Routledge, 1977] 8). Denotation is thus shown to be a product, an effect, of connotation. In brief, denotations and connotations continually switch places, evolve into each other, or disappear completely, depending upon the position of the subject.

16. Compare the quote from Franz Boas with which Claude Lévi-Strauss prefaces "A Structural Study of Myth": "It would seem that mythological worlds have been built up only to be shattered again, and that new worlds were built up from the fragments" (*Structural Anthropology*, trans. Claire Jacobson and Brooke Grundfest Schoepf [New York: Basic, 1963] 206).

17. Richard Chase, *Quest for Myth* (Baton Rouge: Louisiana State UP, 1949) 106.

18. Victoria Hamilton, *Narcissus and Oedipus: The Children of Psychoanalysis* (London: Routledge, 1982).

19. Writers such as Mary Renault and Henry Treece are, of course, exceptions to this general rule. In fact, Treece completely rewrote Oedipus' story in 1964 in his novel *Oedipus*, published in America in 1965 as *The Eagle King*. In this book, Treece introduces a number of changes in Sophocles' version and presents Oedipus as the champion of a progressive patriarchy over the established matriarchy. Because these kinds of prose retellings are not usually associated with the phrase "myth in fiction" (indeed, they are actually new versions of specific myths), they belong to the literary tradition of a myth, not to the type of fiction examined in this study.

20. White calls this coexisting mythic construct a *prefiguration*, because the initial appearance of a myth in a novel "anticipates" the plot (*Mythology in the Modern Novel* 11).

21. Jonathan Culler, *Structuralist Poetics: Structuralism, Linguistics, and the Study of Literature* (Ithaca: Cornell UP, 1975) 116.

22. Ernst Cassirer, *Language and Myth*, trans. Suzanne Langer (New York: Harper, 1946) 91–92.

23. For a review and critique of these systems, see Culler 189–238. Robert Scholes also discusses Greimas, Todorov, Barthes, and Gérard Genette in his *Structuralism in Literature*.

24. As examples of Lévi-Strauss' critics, see Terence Turner, "Narrative Structure and Mythopoesis: A Critique and Reformulation of Structuralist Concepts of Myth, Narrative and Poetics," *Arethusa* 10 (1977): 103–63; Cedric Watts, "King Oedipus and the Toy-vendor," *Reconstructing Literature*, ed. Laurence Lerner (Totowa, NJ: Barnes, 1983) 106–22; Culler 40–54; Scholes, *Structuralism in Literature* 68–74; Albert Cook, *Myth and Language* (Bloomington: Indiana UP, 1980) 13–36; and Rudnytsky 236–50. For a more comprehensive list, see François H. Lapointe and Claire C.

Lapointe, eds., *Claude Lévi-Strauss and His Critics: An International Bibliography of Criticism (1950–1976)* (New York: Garland, 1977); and Joan Nordquist, comp., *Claude Lévi-Strauss: A Bibliography* (Santa Cruz, CA: Reference and Research Services, 1987).

25. Lévi-Strauss 210.

26. For example, Marie Delcourt has proposed that the Oedipus myth comprises six parts, each of which is a common element in other hero myths: the exposed infant, the father murderer, the victor over the monster, the riddle, the marriage to the princess, and the mother union (*Oedipe ou la légende du conquérant* [Paris: Société d'Édition des Belles Lettres, 1944]). Similarly, Richard Fabrizio identifies seven stages—exposure, maturation, confrontation, riddle and Sphinx, incest, punishment, and rebirth—which mark Oedipus' "birth, life, and symbolic existence in the lives of his children" (8).

27. Briefly, Lévi-Strauss seeks the mytheme in a linguistic structure (the sentence), fills that structure with content, and from that content intuits a function that he describes as "relations." However, some specious reasoning is required to carry out this procedure, and "relations" seems such an abstruse or catch-all label that one hardly knows how to apply it in turn. For example, could we add Oedipus' relations with his sons and daughters to Lévi-Strauss' list, and equally important, how would we include such essential events as Oedipus' search for self-knowledge and his exile? As Robert Scholes notes, "Using a term like 'relations' enables Lévi-Strauss to adjust his categories to his material with an unscientific élan that dismays his professional colleagues" (*Structuralism in Literature* 69).

28. Turner, "Narrative Structure" 126.

29. Turner, "Narrative Structure" 132.

30. Scholes, *Structuralism in Literature* 69. Terence Turner's objections to Propp's method are also important to keep in mind:

> Propp's fundamental assumption was that the structure of a tale was essentially identical with the form of the sequence of actions and characters in the story. This approach reduces the relevance of paradigmatic features to the bare minimum necessary to identify characters or events as belonging to one of the highly abstract classes of characters or acts making up the stereotypic sequential pattern of which his model consists. . . . In the jargon of generative grammar, Propp's error was to equate the syntactic structure of the tale with its "surface structure" (Chomsky 1966). ("Narrative Structure" 122)

31. Alan Dundes, "Structuralism and Folklore," *Essays in Folkloristics* (Meerut: Folklore Institute, 1978) 180; rpt. from *Studia Fennica* 20 (1976): 75–93.

32. One way to reduce the chances of idiosyncratic analysis would be to compare different versions of a myth to discover those actions that reappear or those "action slots" that are constantly present even though the action itself might change (e.g., imprisonment and no punishment at all have occupied the same place in the story line as Oedipus' self-blinding, and so that space—response to discovery of a transgression—should be shaped into a mytheme). However, this solution poses a problem for the present study, since I have already specified those reasons why Sophocles' version of the Oedipus myth should be the preferred version. But keeping in mind other versions as we make our "cuts" can help to confirm those cuts and remind us of alternative forms of various mythemes that modern authors might use. Indeed, for someone studying a myth that lacks a canonical version—say, the Heracles myth or the Yellow Woman (Kochinnenako) myth of Keres-speaking Native American tribes in New Mexico—the better method of mythemic analysis might be to describe the mythemes generally (e.g., "The hero commits a transgression" instead of "The hero commits incest") so as to be able to accommodate more easily the myth's many expressions.

2. A Poetics for Myth in Fiction

1. Wolfgang Iser, *The Act of Reading: A Theory of Aesthetic Response,* trans. David Henry Wilson (Baltimore: Johns Hopkins UP, 1978) 107.
2. Umberto Eco, *Semiotics and the Philosophy of Language* (Bloomington: Indiana UP, 1984) 43. Unless otherwise noted, subsequent page references to Eco are to this work and are cited parenthetically within the text.
3. Iser, *Act of Reading* 21. Michael Steig points out that, taken literally, "reader-text interaction, in which *both* sides act, is impossible"; only the reader, not the text, can "act." However, as Steig also observes,

There still may be a phenomenologically sound use for a term like interaction or transaction: to designate a process between the reader and his perceptions of and responses to the text from moment to moment, whether this be linear (relating each additional perception to what has preceded it) or reflective (relating a number of perceptions that have already taken place to form a new perception—an interpretation). For even if the text does not really "act," reading often feels like interaction simply because as one's perceptions change, the text itself seems to change. In all such processes the text is perceived as an "other," no matter how strongly one may be committed to the principle of meaning-in-the-reader. (*Stories of Reading: Subjectivity and Literary Understanding* [Baltimore: Johns Hopkins UP, 1989] 11)

4. By making interest in and familiarity with the myth the distinguishing features of the reader, I am reinforcing my central thesis that I am describing a process of reading. Certainly this approach omits key elements that affect the meaning a person attributes to a text and its mythemes—including socialization, cultural background, value system, and reading experiences—but it has the advantage of applying to a variety of readers encountering and interpreting a variety of myths in a variety of fiction. As I state several times in this study, readers often interpret the same mytheme differently; and I would argue that some (if not most) of their differences of opinion can be traced to variables such as political belief and cultural perspective. Nonetheless, the interaction that leads readers to reach those interpretations is, I believe, essentially the same.

5. *Substantial* is necessarily ambiguous but indicates that the myth has been used generously (quantitatively) as well as to good effect (qualitatively), measurements that the reader-critic must arbitrate. How such arbitration occurs will be discussed throughout this book, especially throughout the rest of this chapter.

6. As Umberto Eco states, "Since the semantic encyclopedia is in itself potentially infinite, semiosis is unlimited, and, from the extreme periphery of a given sememe, the center of any other could be reached, and vice versa" (*The Role of the Reader: Explorations in the Semiotics of Texts* [Bloomington: Indiana UP, 1979] 24).

7. Peter Rabinowitz, *Before Reading: Narrative Conventions and the Politics of Interpretation* (Ithaca: Cornell UP, 1987) 22.

8. Terry Eagleton, qtd. in Rabinowitz 32.

9. George Eliot, *The Mill on the Floss*, ed. Gordon S. Haight (Boston: Houghton, 1961) 117.

10. T. S. Eliot was one of the first to foresee the consequences of Joyce's *Ulysses* for authors, if not for readers:

In using the myth, in manipulating a continuous parallel between contemporaneity and antiquity, Mr Joyce is pursuing a method which others must pursue after him. They will not be imitators, any more than the scientist who uses the discoveries of an Einstein in pursuing his own, independent, further investigations. It is simply a way of controlling, of ordering, of giving a shape and a significance to the immense panorama of futility and anarchy which is contemporary history. ("Ulysses, Order, and Myth," *The Dial* 75 [1923]: 483)

In a reprinting of this essay, Eliot added a note in which he states, "To say that other writers must follow the procedure of *Ulysses* is . . . absurd" ("Myth and Literary Classicism," *The Modern Tradition*, ed. Richard Ellmann and

Charles Feidelson, Jr. [New York: Oxford UP, 1965] 681). Eliot thus recognized the presumptuousness of expressing his prediction as a command (others must pursue this method), but of course, many writers have adopted and varied Joyce's approach. What Lillian Feder says about modern poets and their use of myth pertains also to modern fiction writers:

> [P]oets of our time, influenced by comparative mythology, archeology, anthropology, and psychology, have approached myth differently from their predecessors. Allegory and mythological decoration are rare in serious twentieth-century poetry. There have been, on the other hand, a conscious rejection and an exploitation of the ritual elements in myth and also a general awareness of the psychological implications of mythical tales. Furthermore, poets have consciously attempted to revive myth as a literary device. (*Ancient Myth in Modern Poetry* [Princeton: Princeton UP, 1971] 25)

11. The modern reader's understanding of the possibilities for myth in fiction leads to an interesting situation. Just as we are aware that a twentieth-century story referring to a myth might use that myth in the extended way of Joyce or Mann, so also does our familiarity with this method affect our relationship to earlier fiction. We could, for example, determine that Mr. Tulliver's Oedipal connection is more than just an authorial aside and that the authorial reading is therefore insufficient. Such a determination depends, of course, on recovering other, more substantial evidence of the myth, evidence that Eliot might not have deliberately included in her novel but that still might be present. Although I do not find such evidence in *The Mill on the Floss*, I mention the possibility here since such a search can prove productive for pre-twentieth-century fiction, as we will see in chapter 3 with H. G. Wells' *The Time Machine* and Jules Verne's *An Antarctic Mystery*. It is also worth noting that this ability to discern myth throughout a nineteenth- or eighteenth-century narrative does not imply that one is reading anachronistically or torturing the text into saying something it never meant. Rather, such an ability demonstrates a major point of this study: myth can become implicitly embedded in fiction. When this happens, it functions like a language, but to do so, it needs someone who has learned that language and can read and interpret its signs. But here I am referring to mythemes and am getting ahead of myself. This subject will be taken up in the next two sections.

12. White, *Mythology in the Modern Novel* 12.

13. Max Frisch's *Homo Faber* provides an example of an Oedipal reference appearing late in the narrative. Almost two-thirds of the way into the novel, Oedipus' name surfaces when Hanna, an archeologist and the mother

of Walter Faber's daughter, speaks to Faber about myths. She points to Oedipus and the Sphinx, "portrayed in childlike fashion on a broken vase" (trans. Michael Bullock [New York: Harcourt, 1959] 146). Subsequent page references to this novel are cited parenthetically within the text. As I discuss in chapter 5, Frisch's narrative has contained several implicit Oedipal mythemes up to this point, but here is the first explicit hint that Oedipus is known to both Frisch and Faber. It confirms that the parallels readers have been drawing between Faber and Oedipus are part of the authorial reading and encourages them to continue seeking such correspondences.

14. White, *Mythology in the Modern Novel* 119–20.

15. Peter Brooks, *Reading for the Plot* (1984; New York: Vintage, 1985) 280. Another helpful description of the retrospective action in the reading process can be found in Menakhem Perry's "Literary Dynamics: How the Order of a Text Creates Its Meanings, with an Analysis of Faulkner's 'A Rose for Emily,'" *Poetics Today* 1.1–2 (1979): 58–61. Other related discussions and terms include: E. D. Hirsch's idea about the activity of reading being the process of developing "corrigible schemata" (*The Aims of Interpretation* [Chicago: U of Chicago P, 1976] 33–34); Barbara Herrnstein Smith's notion of "retrospective patterning" (*Poetic Closure: A Study of How Poems End* [Chicago: U of Chicago P, 1968]); and James Phelan's several examinations of the relations between beginnings, middles, and ends, most recently in *Reading People, Reading Plots: Character, Progression, and the Interpretation of Narrative* (Chicago: U of Chicago P, 1989).

16. Michel Butor, *Passing Time*, trans. Jean Stewart (London: Faber, 1961; London: Calder, 1965) 145. Subsequent page references to this novel are cited parenthetically within the text.

17. This equation has behind it a history of debate. Early explicators of the sign presumed that it consisted of its expression and the thing it named. Today, the view is slightly more sophisticated as Scholes points out:

> The most powerful assumption in French semiotic thought since Saussure has been the notion that a sign consists not of a name and the object it refers to, but of a sound-image and a concept, a signifier and a signified. Saussure, as amplified by Roland Barthes and others, has taught us to recognize an unbridgeable gap between words and things, signs and referents. The whole notion of "sign and referent" has been rejected by the French structuralists and their followers as too materialistic and simpleminded. Signs do not refer to things, they signify concepts, and concepts are aspects of thought, not of reality. (*Semiotics and Interpretation* [New Haven: Yale UP, 1982] 23–24)

See also Terence Hawkes, *Structuralism and Semiotics* (London: Methuen, 1977) 25.

18. In *The Role of the Reader*, Eco applies the process of abduction to the entire act of reading in a similar but much more comprehensive way than I have in this chapter. He maintains that the text establishes a "topic" or "topics" either through excessive repetition or strategic location. In the latter case, "the sensitive reader, feeling something unusual in the *dispositio*, tries to make abductions (that is, to single out a hidden rule or regularity) and to test them in the course of his further reading. That is why in reading literary texts one is obliged to look backward many times, and, in general, the more complex the text, the more it has to be read twice, and the second time from the end" (26).

19. The reader's situation in *Passing Time* is much more complicated than is indicated by the brief descriptions provided here and earlier in this chapter. Since Revel has connected his dilemma to that of Theseus and that of Cain, but never consciously to that of Oedipus, these three myths surface in different ways in the narrative, intersecting at several points, and causing a variety of exchanges among themselves and between themselves and the novel. I will provide more detail about this interaction and how the Oedipus myth finally eclipses the other two as paradigm in the fourth chapter.

20. For a thorough discussion of how authors motivate a mythic analogy through characters, see chapter 4 of White's *Mythology in the Modern Novel*, esp. 141–49. White notes that it is easier to motivate such comparisons when the character is an intellectual and/or an artist.

21. Alberto Moravia, *The Lie*, trans. Angus Davidson (New York: Farrar, 1966) 62–63. Subsequent page references to this novel are cited parenthetically within the text.

22. Later Francesco will restore this aspect when he expands the corruption affecting his life to the malaise of all Romans, their symptoms consisting of "the imperceptible, unceasing, natural movement of senseless, non-genuine everyday life" (279).

23. The only principal family relationship that the Oedipus myth seems incapable of absorbing is that between brother and sister. The lines of attraction are definitely drawn along a vertical axis rather than a horizontal one. James B. Twitchell observes that the motivation and consequence of parental incest and sibling incest are so different that each probably deserves a separate name and category (*Forbidden Partners: The Incest Taboo in Modern Culture* [New York: Columbia UP, 1987] xiii). Interestingly, and in possible contradiction to this suggestion, one of the modern analogues for the Oedipus myth is the story of Pope Gregory, whose most heinous sin was to commit incest with his sister. For a survey of mythic names given to psychoanalytic complexes, see Roy Huss, "Appendix B: The 'Complexes' of Art: Some Contributions Made by Myth and Literature to the Language of

Psychoanalysis," *The Mindscapes of Art: Dimensions of the Psyche in Fiction, Drama, and Film* (Rutherford: Fairleigh Dickinson UP, 1986) 186–201.

24. Alfred Messer, "The 'Phaedra Complex,'" *Archives of General Psychiatry* 21 (1969): 213–18; mentioned by Twitchell 262n10. Consider also J. J. Putnam's invention of the term *Griselda complex* to describe the father's unconscious sexual involvement with his daughter and Arpad Pauncz's related term the *Lear complex* (referred to by Huss 190). According to Otto Rank, "the second great complex" has for its contents "the erotic relations between father and daughter" (*The Myth of the Birth of the Hero: A Psychological Interpretation of Mythology*, trans. F. Robbins and Smith Ely Jelliffe [1909; New York: Journal of Nervous and Mental Disease Pub. Co., 1914] 77).

25. As Twitchell relates the statistics: "Father-daughter or surrogate father-figure incest is the most prevalent (approximately 70 percent), then brother-sister, including adopted or 'rem' siblings (20 percent), and the remainder is uncle-niece or in-law activity, and finally in much smaller numbers mother-son (which has not been explained by the Freudians, who made oedipal dynamics so important)" (13). See also Judith Herman and Lisa Hirschman, "Father-Daughter Incest," *Signs: Journal of Women in Culture and Society* 2.4 (1977): 735–56; and Elizabeth Janeway, "Incest: A Rational Look at the Oldest Taboo," *Ms.* 10 (1981): 61+.

26. For a good overview of biological, psychological, and sociological positions on incest, see Twitchell 243–59.

27. Freud elaborated on this obsession two years later in "On the Universal Tendency to Debasement in the Sphere of Love (Contributions to the Psychology of Love, II) (1912)." Both essays can be found in volume 11 of *The Standard Edition of the Complete Psychological Works of Sigmund Freud*, trans. and ed. James Strachey (London: Hogarth, 1957).

28. Nancy Chodorow, *The Reproduction of Mothering: Psychoanalysis and the Sociology of Gender* (Berkeley: U of California P, 1978) esp. 180–90, "Mothering, Masculinity, and Capitalism"; and Christiane Olivier, *Jocasta's Children: The Imprint of the Mother*, trans. George Craig (London: Routledge, 1989).

29. Twitchell 255.

30. Rudnytsky 16.

31. Edward Said, *Beginnings: Intention and Method* (New York: Basic, 1975) 170.

32. In *Studies on Hysteria* (1895), Freud refers to the "blindness of the seeing eye" to describe that "strange state of mind in which one knows and does not know a thing at the same time" (*Standard Edition* 2:117); pointed out by Rudnytsky 21.

33. For example, E. R. Dodds argues, "But we are not entitled to blame Oedipus either for carelessness in failing to compile a handlist [of all the things he must not do, specifically quarrel with men older than himself and sleep with older women] or for lack of self-control in failing to obey its injunctions. For no such possibilities are mentioned in the play, or even hinted at; and it is an essential critical principle that *what is not mentioned in the play does not exist*" ("On Misunderstanding the *Oedipus Rex*," *The Ancient Concept of Progress and Other Essays on Greek Literature and Belief* [Oxford: Oxford UP, 1973] 68). Here Dodds seems to be echoing Aristotle, who, in *The Poetics*, claims that the several illogicalities of *Oedipus the King* occur outside the play and are thus, one infers, not subject to evaluation. But not all scholars agree with Dodds, or Aristotle, that we cannot evaluate what is "outside" the play. Frederick Ahl, for example, takes issue with Dodds, asking, "Can one know which questions the dramatist did not intend us to ask?" (*Sophocles' Oedipus: Evidence and Self-Conviction* [Ithaca: Cornell UP, 1991] 5).

34. Philip Vellacott, *Sophocles and Oedipus: A Study of* Oedipus Tyrannus *with a New Translation* (Ann Arbor: U of Michigan P, 1971) 119.

35. Rudnytsky 270–71.

36. Lacan's reading of Oedipus is not an extended argument but is scattered throughout his lectures. Two of the best sources for understanding his views on Oedipus are Anthony Wilden's notes and commentary in "Lacan and the Discourse of the Other," in Lacan's *Speech and Language in Psychoanalysis*, trans. Anthony Wilden (1968; Baltimore: Johns Hopkins UP, 1981) esp. 96, 168; and Shoshana Felman's "Beyond Oedipus: The Specimen Story of Psychoanalysis," chap. 5, *Jacques Lacan and the Adventure of Insight: Psychoanalysis in Contemporary Culture* (Cambridge: Harvard UP, 1987) 98–159. Felman reminds us that, for Lacan, Oedipus' true assumption of his destiny comes in *Oedipus at Colonus*, not *Oedipus the King*. Hence, Oedipus' recognition is not complete until his death. For more on Lacan's interpretation of Oedipus, see my discussion in chapter 5.

37. Hans Blumenberg, *Work on Myth*, trans. Robert M. Wallace (Cambridge: MIT P, 1985) 277.

38. Hoffman 154.

39. Hoffman 154.

40. Rosemary Davies, "The Mother as Destroyer: Psychic Division in the Writings of D. H. Lawrence," *The D. H. Lawrence Review* 13 (1980): 220–38.

41. Giles Mitchell, "*Sons and Lovers* and the Oedipal Project," *The D. H. Lawrence Review* 13 (1980): 209–19.

42. Flannery O'Connor, *Wise Blood, Three By Flannery O'Connor: Wise Blood, A Good Man Is Hard to Find, The Violent Bear It Away* (New

York: NAL, n.d.) 121. Subsequent page references to this novel are cited parenthetically within the text.

43. John Lewis Longley, Jr., "Joe Christmas: The Hero in the Modern World," *The Tragic Mask: A Study of Faulkner's Heroes* (Chapel Hill: U of North Carolina P, 1957) 194–95.

44. Readers often describe Sophocles' *Oedipus the King* as a "tragedy of fate," perhaps because Freud interpreted it as such, so it is worth noting that this is not the consensus of scholars of the play. Bernard Knox, to cite just one example, argues that "in the play which Sophocles wrote the hero's will is absolutely free and he is fully responsible for the catastrophe" (*Oedipus at Thebes* [New Haven: Yale UP, 1957] 5).

45. William Faulkner, "Session Nine," *Faulkner in the University: Class Conferences at the University of Virginia 1957–1958*, ed. Frederick L. Gwynn and Joseph L. Blotner (1959; New York: Vintage, 1965) 72.

46. Longley 204.

47. For example, in "Faulkner's Theban Saga: *Light in August*," I argue that the primary mytheme of Faulkner's novel is the patricide one, a reading that is informed by Erich Fromm's analysis of the Oedipus myth as depicting the ancient fight between the patriarchal and matriarchal systems of society. Joe Christmas is like Oedipus, I conclude, in that he too fights social arrangements that frustrate the individual's drive for autonomy and self-fulfillment and, in so doing, comes to embody both the corruption of the past and the possibilities for the future (*The Southern Literary Journal* 18.1 [1985]: 13–29).

48. Frank Baldanza, "The Classicism of Alberto Moravia," *Modern Fiction Studies* 3 (1957): 310, 311.

49. Frank Baldanza, "Mature Moravia," *Contemporary Literature* 9 (1968): 507–21.

50. Righter 64–65.

3. The Power of the Solitary Mytheme: The Anti-Sphinx of Alternative Wastelands

1. Casey Fredericks, *The Future of Eternity: Mythologies of Science Fiction and Fantasy* (Bloomington: Indiana UP, 1982) 8. Subsequent page references to this work are cited parenthetically within the text.

2. Knox 117. See also V. Ehrenberg, *Sophocles and Pericles* (Oxford: Oxford UP, 1954).

3. Actually, two other mythemes also reappear in various science fiction works: the murder of the father (7) and incest with the mother (9). As the

cornerstones of Freud's theories about the family, these two mythemes form part of a psychoanalytic stream within science fiction. This stream arises, or develops its strongest currents, around 1950, when the so-called New Wave writers shifted the arena explored by the genre from external to internal space and identified this redirection as "speculative fiction." Such "interiorization" entailed a consciousness of psychoanalytic theory; and Freudian, as well as Jungian, ideas began to supply a sort of secondary mythos from which the science fiction author could draw. Among such works are Robert Heinlein's *Time Enough for Love* (1973), where the adult protagonist travels back to the time and place of his childhood and makes love to his mother; and Philip José Farmer's *Night of Light* (1966), where the hero's "desire for an unresponsive mother leads to murderous thoughts not just about his father, but about the whole family" (Mary T. Brizzi, *Philip José Farmer* [Mercer Island, WA: Starmont, 1980] 31). However, as interesting as these plot twists might be, their primary source is Freud, not Sophocles. The entire disposition of the incest and patricide mythemes in these stories comes from the Oedipus complex rather than the Oedipus myth. Put another way, these novels are actually structured around a second-order myth (Freud's interpretation of Oedipus) rather than the Oedipus myth itself. Strictly speaking, then, they are outside the range of this study.

4. Neither Verne nor Wells identified his work as science fiction. The former used the term *scientific fiction*, the latter *scientific romance*. Still, these two men have often been credited with giving form to the science fiction genre, and their own designations have often given way to the more generic term.

5. H. G. Wells, *The Definitive* Time Machine: *A Critical Edition of H. G. Wells's Scientific Romance*, ed. Harry M. Geduld (Bloomington: Indiana UP, 1987) 44–45, italics mine. Subsequent page references to this novel are cited parenthetically within the text.

6. See, for example, David Ketterer, "Oedipus as Time Traveller," *Science-Fiction Studies* 9 (1982): 340; and Catherine Rainwater, "Encounters with the 'White Sphinx': Poe's Influence on Some Early Works of H. G. Wells," *English Literature in Transition* 26.1 (1983): 39.

7. Jane Harrison notes that the Sphinx "was mainly a local Theban bogey, but she became the symbol of oracular divinity," and in time, "the savage 'man-snatching' aspect of the Sphinx faded, remembered only in the local legend, while her oracular aspect grew" (*Prolegomena to the Study of Greek Religion*, 2nd ed. [Cambridge: Cambridge UP, 1908] 210). As I will discuss shortly, Wells' White Sphinx also has a "man-snatching" side.

8. Francis Bacon, qtd. in Frank Scafella, "The White Sphinx and *The Time Machine*," *Science-Fiction Studies* 8 (1981): 255.

9. Erich Neumann, *The Origins and History of Consciousness*, trans.

R. F. C. Hull, Bollingen Series 42 (Princeton: Princeton UP, 1970) 161. Subsequent page references to this work are cited parenthetically within the text.

10. Harry M. Geduld's collection of terms used by the Time Traveller to describe the Morlocks reveals just how intensely he loathes them and also how language enables him to distance himself from them. Such terms include "human spider," "the little monster," "this bleached, obscene nocturnal Thing," "this new vermin," "They were just the half-bleached colour of . . . worms . . . they were filthily cold to the touch," "nauseatingly inhuman," "ant-like," "human rats," "helpless abominations," and "damned souls" (Wells, *The Definitive* Time Machine 107n28).

11. David Lake, "The White Sphinx and the Whitened Lemur: Images of Death in *The Time Machine*," *Science-Fiction Studies* 6 (1979): 79.

12. Bernard Bergonzi, *The Early H. G. Wells: A Study of the Scientific Romances* (Manchester: Manchester UP, 1961) 56.

13. Lake 79.

14. Many of the similarities that I list here between the Morlocks and the Time Traveller have been noted by other critics, particularly Mark Hennelly, Jr., in "*The Time Machine*: A Romance of 'The Human Heart,'" *Extrapolation* 20 (1979): 154–67, who argues that Wells' novel should be read as a romance in which the scientific is simply an externalization of the psychological. Wells pleads, Hennelly believes, "for recognizing the essential, paradoxical unity of a well-balanced and whole personality system" (159). The Time Traveller's task is thus to admit the Morlock side of himself and integrate it with "his more deeply suppressed Eloi side" (164). While I agree with Hennelly's basic premise, I obviously have a different view about the Time Traveller's psychological makeup, positing the Eloi as his conscious side, the Morlocks as his repressed unconscious.

15. Significantly, in "Human Evolution, an Artificial Process," an article published the year after *The Time Machine*, Wells writes that civilized man is a compound of "an inherited factor, the natural man, . . . the culminating ape" (what I am calling primitive man) and "an acquired factor, the artificial man, the highly plastic creature of tradition, suggestion, and reasoned thought" (*Early Writings in Science and Science Fiction by H. G. Wells*, ed. Robert M. Philmus and David Y. Hughes [Berkeley: U of California P, 1975] 217; qtd. in Hennelly 163).

16. Lake 77–78.

17. John Huntington, *The Logic of Fantasy: H. G. Wells and Science Fiction* (New York: Columbia UP, 1982) 45.

18. Roslynn Haynes, *H. G. Wells: Discoverer of the Future: The Influence of Science on His Thought* (London: Macmillan, 1980) 22.

19. Thomas H. Huxley, qtd. in Huntington 177n7.

20. Rainwater 39. Rainwater's perceptive argument concerning *The Time Machine* closely resembles the one I am making here, but like other critics, Rainwater misses the fact that the Sphinx, too, is one of the Time Traveller's projections.

21. Sophocles, *The Theban Plays*, trans. E. F. Watling (New York: Penguin, 1947) 26. Subsequent page references to Sophocles' Theban plays are cited parenthetically within the text.

22. Compare Euripides in *The Phoenician Women*, who has Antigone say, "and the ruin began / when he unriddled the riddling song / of the singing Sphinx and slew her dead" (*Euripides V*, trans. Elizabeth Wycoff [Chicago: Phoenix-U of Chicago P, 1959] 129).

23. Strictly measured, Verne's novel might not be considered science fiction. Nevertheless, *An Antarctic Mystery* exhibits characteristics normally associated with science fiction—namely, the voyage to an unknown, unexplored land, which involves the characters in a number of fantastic but plausible experiences. Significantly, several critics have also proposed that Poe's "The Narrative of A. Gordon Pym," the inspiration for Verne's story, be viewed, to some degree, as science fiction (see, for instance, J. M. Santraud, "Dans le sillage de la baleinière d'Arthur Gordon Pym: *Le sphinx des glaces, Dan Yack*," *Etudes Anglaises* 25 [1972]: 353).

24. Jules Verne, *An Antarctic Mystery*, trans. Mrs. Cashel Hoey (Philadelphia: Lippincott, 1899; Boston: Hall, 1975) 323–24. Subsequent page references to this novel are cited parenthetically within the text.

25. Edgar Fawcett's poem "Oedipus and the Sphinx," published in 1902, three years after the English translation of Verne's novel, provides an interesting contrast to what Joerling says here. In this poem the Sphinx is aligned with superstition which Oedipus, the representative of science, slays. However, Fawcett's Sphinx understands the consequences of this victory. As she tells Oedipus,

> Thou,
> Science, assaulter of the Unknowable
> Until it yields its ultimate secret, thou
> Must suffer, and with exorbitance of pain,
> This being the doom of all who fight to tear
> From nature, deity, what thou wilt, its mask,
> Of incommunicable reserve—
> (*North American Review* 175 [1902]: 875)

Exactly how Oedipus-Science must suffer, the Sphinx does not explain; but she at least recognizes, as Joerling does not, that knowledge has its price.

26. For analyses of numerous flood stories, see the essays collected by Alan Dundes in *The Flood Myth* (Berkeley: U of California P, 1988).

27. Philip José Farmer, *Venus on the Half-Shell* (New York: Dell, 1974) 191. Subsequent page references to this novel, published under the pseudonym Kilgore Trout, by way of Kurt Vonnegut, are cited parenthetically within the text.

28. Philip José Farmer, "Riders of the Purple Wage: Or the Great Gavage," *Dangerous Visions: 33 Original Stories*, ed. Harlan Ellison (Garden City, NY: Doubleday, 1967) 59. Subsequent page references to this story are cited parenthetically within the text.

29. Philip Dick and Roger Zelazny, *Deus Irae* (New York: Dell, 1976) 99. Subsequent page references to this novel are cited parenthetically within the text.

30. In fact, even Verne's novel—which is far from dystopian, exalting as it does scientific progress and the humanitarian spirit—locates its Sphinx at the barren and cold Antarctic Pole. Still, Verne tempers this desolation by stressing the wonders of nature more than the physical details of the landscape.

31. Casey Fredericks, "Revivals of Ancient Mythologies in Current Science Fiction and Fantasy," *Many Futures, Many Worlds: Theme and Form in Science Fiction*, ed. Thomas D. Clareson (Kent, OH: Kent State UP, 1977) 53.

4. Mythemes and Questions of Genre: The Blindness of the Private Eye in Antidetective Fiction

1. Tzvetan Todorov, "The Typology of Detective Fiction," *The Poetics of Prose*, trans. Richard Howard (Ithaca: Cornell UP, 1977) 43.

2. To cite only one example of each group, E. R. Dodds writes, in an essay intended to correct major misconceptions about Sophocles' tragedy, that "despite certain similarities, the *Oedipus Rex* is not a detective story but a dramatized folktale. If we insist on reading it as if it were a law report we must expect to miss the point" (68). In contrast, Jan R. Van Meter condemns the critical prejudice against the detective genre, which is so great that scholars forget that *Crime and Punishment* and *Bleak House* are essentially detective novels. Van Meter argues that the detective story is one of the oldest forms of literature, *Oedipus the King* being the first, and claims that the myth underlying it—the search for the self existing on the fringes of the legitimate—is central to our culture ("Sophocles and the Rest of the Boys in the Pulps: Myth and the Detective Novel," *Dimensions of*

Detective Fiction, ed. Larry N. Landrum, Pat Browne, and Ray B. Browne [n.p.: Popular, 1976] 12–21).

    3. Stefano Tani, *The Doomed Detective: The Contribution of the Detective Novel to Postmodern American and Italian Fiction* (Carbondale: Southern Illinois UP, 1984) 34. Subsequent page references to this book are cited parenthetically within the text. Others who have studied the antidetective story, sometimes called the metaphysical detective story, include Michael Holquist, "Whodunit and Other Questions: Metaphysical Detective Stories in Post-War Fiction," *New Literary History* 3 (1971): 135–56; and William V. Spanos, "The Detective and the Boundary: Some Notes on the Postmodern Literary Imagination," *Boundary* 1 (1972): 147–68.

    4. Todorov 44.

    5. As Tani points out, the duality of murderer and sleuth has been a component of detective fiction ever since Edgar Allan Poe formalized the genre in April 1841 with the publication of "The Murders in the Rue Morgue" (1–15). The retention of separate personalities, the rational detective meeting his irrational alter ego in the criminal, has governed the type for over a century. However, Martin Priestman lists several "classic" detective stories that "either contravene this separation of functions or actively play with it"— for example, Wilkie Collins' *The Moonstone,* where Franklin Blake combines elements of victim, detective, and criminal; and Arthur Conan Doyle's "The Final Problem," where Sherlock Holmes becomes "at once murderer and victim" (19). Priestman argues that such works demonstrate the "limitations of *a priori* assumptions about the formula" and are marked by a tendency to "'make you think,' to raise the stakes of the game" (19). Nonetheless, he believes that the formula exists and suggests that although *Oedipus the King* provides a bridge between detective fiction and tragedy, it does not cross that boundary, partly *because* it combines the functions of the detective and criminal in one person (*Detective Fiction and Literature: The Figure on the Carpet* [London: Macmillan, 1990] 18–19).

    6. Consider, for example, the fourth entry of S. S. Van Dine (the creator of detective Philo Vance) on his list, compiled in 1928, of twenty rules for detective authors: "The detective himself, or one of the official investigators, should never turn out to be the culprit. This is bald trickery, on a par with offering some one a bright penny for a five-dollar gold piece. It's false pretenses" (first appeared in the *American Magazine* Sept. 1928; rpt. in *The Art of the Mystery Story,* ed. Howard Haycraft [New York: Simon, 1946] 190). Ronald A. Knox repeated the admonition in his Ten Commandments of Detection, which was incorporated into his introduction to *The Best [English] Detective Stories of 1928,* asserting, "*The detective must not himself commit the crime.*" He added, however, that this applies "only where

the author personally vouches for the statement that the detective *is* a detective" (rpt. in Haycraft 196).

7. See George Grella, "Murder and Manners: The Formal Detective Novel," *Novel* 4 (1970): 45.

8. Spanos 154.

9. Bruce Morrissette, "Oedipus and Existentialism: *Les Gommes* of Robbe-Grillet," *Wisconsin Studies in Contemporary Literature* 1 (1960); rev. and rpt. as "Oedipus or the Closed Circle: *The Erasers* (1953)," in Morrissette's *The Novels of Robbe-Grillet*, trans. Morrissette (Ithaca: Cornell UP, 1975) 38–74. Unless otherwise noted, subsequent page references are to the Cornell reprinting of this essay and are cited parenthetically within the text.

10. Jean Ricardou, qtd. in Ann Jefferson, *The Nouveau Roman and the Poetics of Fiction* (Cambridge: Cambridge UP, 1980) 19.

11. Alain Robbe-Grillet, *The Erasers*, trans. Richard Howard (New York: Grove, 1964) 32. Subsequent page references to this novel are cited parenthetically within the text.

12. Robert Brock, "Robbe-Grillet's *Les Gommes* and Graham Greene's *This Gun For Hire*: Imitation or Initiation," *Modern Fiction Studies* 29 (1983): 689. Other critics have also argued that we have no proof that Dupont is Wallas' son; see especially Olga Bernal, who states, "Mais, précisément, c'est un contresens, un hasard, et notre besoin de récupérer la mort en la transformant en un parricide est ici délibérément contrarié. Nous n'avons aucune preuve que Wallas soit le fils de Dupont et l'ordre du roman veut que nous n'en ayons pas" ("But, exactly, it is a misinterpretation, a mistake, and our need to recover death in transforming it into a patricide is here deliberately made the opposite. We have no proof that Wallas was the son of Dupont and the plot wants us not to have any") (*Alain Robbe-Grillet: le roman de l'absence* [Paris: Gallimard, 1964] 67). But the list of critics who have adopted Morrissette's view is surprisingly long. It includes Victor Brombert, "A Victim Was Waiting," *New York Times Book Review* 18 Oct. 1964: 4; A. R. Chadwick and Virginia Harger-Grinling, "Mythic Structures in Alain Robbe-Grillet's *Les Gommes*," *International Fiction Review* 2 (1984): 103; J. M. Cocking, "The 'Nouveau Roman' in France," *Essays in French Literature* 2 (1965): 1–14; Vivian Mercier, *The New Novel: From Queneau to Pinget* (New York: Farrar, 1971) 30; Ben Stoltzfus, *Alain Robbe-Grillet and the New French Novel* (Carbondale: Southern Illinois UP, 1964) 75; John Sturrock, *The French New Novel: Claude Simon, Michel Butor, Alain Robbe-Grillet* (London: Oxford UP, 1969) 190, 197, 225; and George Szanto, *Narrative Consciousness: Structure and Perception in the Fiction of Kafka, Beckett, and Robbe-Grillet* (Austin: U of Texas P, 1972) 135, 143, 146. In

his 1960 version of his essay, Morrissette notes that one reviewer of *Les Gommes*, Jean-Michel Royer, anticipated him by identifying the relationship between Dupont and Wallas as father-son (72n9).

13. This interview follows Kathleen O'Neill's "On *Passing Time*," *Mosaic* 8 (1974): 35, 37.

14. John White, for example, asserts that the Oedipal prefiguration in *Passing Time* is far less important than the counterbalanced images of Theseus and Cain, and he criticizes Jean Roudaut (*Michel Butor ou le livre futur* [Paris: Gallimard, 1964] 163 ff.) for overstressing the Oedipus myth (*Mythology in the Modern Novel* 212n34). To be fair, in his more recent article, White somewhat alters this position, stating that Revel becomes his own Sherlock Holmes and Oedipus at the same time and that "the more the temporal [labyrinth] begins to dominate the story, the more insistently the reader is presented with the Oedipal prefiguration" ("Mythological Fiction" 88).

15. Jefferson 34.

16. Peter Cooper, *Signs and Symptoms: Thomas Pynchon and the Contemporary World* (Berkeley: U of California P, 1983) 151.

17. Tony Tanner, *Thomas Pynchon* (London: Methuen, 1982) 60.

18. Thomas Pynchon, *The Crying of Lot 49* (New York: Bantam, 1966) 1. Subsequent page references to this novel are cited parenthetically within the text.

19. Edward Mendelson, "The Sacred, the Profane, and *The Crying of Lot 49*," *Pynchon: A Collection of Critical Essays*, ed. Mendelson (Englewood Cliffs, NJ: Prentice, 1978) 118.

20. See, for example, Robert N. Watson, "Who Bids for Tristero? The Conversion of Pynchon's Oedipa Maas," *Southern Humanities Review* 17 (1983): 59–75, who contends that Pynchon has made it clear that Oedipa will be the one to bid for Lot 49.

21. James Dean Young asserts that Oedipa is not so much more than Oedipus as too much ("The Enigma Variations of Thomas Pynchon," *Critique: Studies in Modern Fiction* 10.1 [1967]: 72); and Caesar observes that, voiced with appropriate emphasis, Oedipa Maas sound like "Oedipus my ass." This Oedipa, Caesar concludes, "is no Oedipus, or only one at the earnest reader's peril" ("A Note on Pynchon's Naming," *Pynchon Notes* 5 [1981]: 5).

22. In *The Doomed Detective*, Tani identifies William Hjortsberg's *Falling Angel* (1978)—made into the movie *Angel Heart*, with Mickey Rourke and Lisa Bonet—as an antidetective novel using the Oedipus myth. Certainly Hjortsberg's novel turns upon the Oedipal mytheme in which the detective discovers he is the criminal, and it also throws in the incest mytheme for good measure. Nevertheless, it does not seem to deserve the

antidetective status that Tani assigns it, and its difference from the other novels we have studied in this chapter helps to confirm the connections of *Oedipus the King* to the postmodern antidetective genre.

In *Falling Angel*, detective Harry Angel is hired by Louis Cyphre to locate Johnny Favorite, a Frank Sinatra-like star popular before World War II and also a war veteran, who has disappeared from a private hospital in upper New York state. Unmistakable coincidences between his own life and that of Favorite, supported by a series of symbolic dreams, convince (or remind) Angel that he is Johnny Favorite, now possessing the name and soul of a young soldier he killed in an attempt to escape the devil with whom he had made a pact. As Tani puts it, Angel solves the crime of his own existence (102–3), yet the denouement of *Falling Angel* does not present us with the metaphysics of relativism and indeterminacy found in *The Erasers, Passing Time*, and *The Crying of Lot 49*. The final scene of Hjortsberg's novel reveals Angel acknowledging that Cyphre *is* the Devil to whom he, as Johnny Favorite, sold his soul, and so the premise of the book becomes that of Ira Levin's *Rosemary's Baby* (1968) or William Blatty's *The Exorcist* (1971): the Devil exists and operates among us.

Furthermore, such metaphysics cannot allow Angel to suffer any of the soul-searching endured by antidetectives like Revel and Oedipa—nor of their predecessor, Oedipus. Epiphany Proudfoot, Angel-Favorite's daughter and lover, relates that "Johnny Favorite was as close to true evil" as her mother ever wanted to come. We would hardly expect such a man to be appalled at the knowledge, suddenly restored, that he has committed crimes against God and society. Nor does Angel feel disoriented or compromised at the end of the quest, as do Wallas, Revel, and Oedipa. He knows his adversary and simply gives himself up to justice here and in the hereafter. There are no alternative answers, no missing clues, no other reality—for either Angel or the reader.

23. R. G. A. Buxton, "Blindness and Limits: Sophocles and the Logic of Myth," *Journal of Hellenic Studies* 100 (1980): 35.

24. Buxton 36.

25. Dodds 76–77.

5. Reading Myths and Mythemes after Freud: From Oedipal Incest to Oedipal Insight

1. As Teresa de Lauretis reminds us, Freud never used the word *desire*; his term *wunsch* corresponds rather to *wish*. However, Lacan does use *desire*, attempting to reorientate Freud's doctrine around this notion (*Alice*

Doesn't: Feminism, Semiotics, Cinema [Bloomington: Indiana UP, 1984] 181), and this is the term that is commonly used in post-Freudian analysis.

2. The word *typically* is carefully chosen in this sentence, for not all of Freud's critics engage in a close rereading of the Oedipus myth. However, they do usually draw upon the myth to support their theories or to repudiate Freud's. Occasionally, they simply draw us to the myth by the novelty of their ideas. For example, Gilles Deleuze and Félix Guattari (*Anti-Oedipus: Capitalism and Schizophrenia*, trans. Robert Hurley, Mark Seem, and Helen R. Lane [New York: Viking, 1977]) do not actually work out their attack on the "familialism" of psychoanalysis by returning to Sophocles' plays. Yet in arguing that Freud's view of desire is reductive (the Oedipus complex "triangulates the unconscious"), they force us to ask whether Freud has accounted for Oedipus' entire experience. Statements such as "There is no Oedipal triangle: Oedipus is always open in an open social field" (96), impressionistic as they are, return us to the myth—if only in quest of confirmation.

3. Such an increase in the semantic encyclopedias of the patricide and incest mythemes has had another consequence for readers. It has destabilized Freud's reading of these mythemes, thus reducing the threat that his reading would overcode them. Much of their semiotic power has thus been restored, and they have regained their ability to enter into relationships with other Oedipal mythemes. As a result, even family romances that have been read from a strictly Freudian position—such as Lawrence's *Sons and Lovers*—are being reexamined from angles provided by alternative interpretations of the incest and patricide mythemes (see chap. 2, 35–36).

4. André Green, *The Tragic Effect: The Oedipus Complex in Tragedy*, trans. Alan Sheridan (Cambridge: Cambridge UP, 1979) 190.

5. Sigmund Freud, *The Interpretation of Dreams*, trans. and ed. James Strachey (New York: Avon, 1965) 295.

6. Consider: Sophie Lazarsfeld, "Did Oedipus Have an Oedipus Complex?" *American Journal of Orthopsychiatry* 14 (1944): 226–29; Heinz Politzer, "Hatte Odipus einen Odipus-Komplex?" *Psychologie in der Litteraturwissenschaft*, ed. W. Paulsen (Heidelberg: Stiehm, 1971) 115–39; and D. Z. Phillips, "What the Complex Did to Oedipus," *Through a Darkening Glass: Philosophy, Literature, and Cultural Change* (Notre Dame: U of Notre Dame P, 1982) 82–88.

7. In fact, a big difference is whether they accept or reject Freud's idea of the Oedipus complex. I want to make clear that I am not suggesting that psychoanalysts like Lacan and Rudnytsky have rejected that concept, for certainly they have not—although Lacan, at least, has revised it considerably. My point is that they have foregrounded another part of the myth—and of Freud's interpretation of it—for explaining the psychoanalytic situation. It

is this shift of attention—from parrincest desire to defense—that is shared by the writers examined in this chapter.

8. For good discussions of Lacan's terminology and theories, see Wilden, "Lacan and the Discourse of the Other"; Ellie Ragland-Sullivan, *Jacques Lacan and the Philosophy of Psychoanalysis* (Urbana: U of Illinois P, 1986); and Juliet Flower MacCannell, *Figuring Lacan: Criticism and the Cultural Unconscious* (London: Croom Helm, 1986).

9. Jacques Lacan, *Le Séminaire, livre II: Le moi dans la théorie de Frued et dans la technique psychoanalytique* (Paris: Seuil, 1978) 58; qtd. in Felman 129–30. Lacan never prepared a systematic account of his interpretation of Oedipus, but Felman's essay, first published in a different form in *Modern Language Notes*, surveys many of Lacan's separate writings on this subject. It is, therefore, one of the best sources for Lacan's ideas about Sophocles' and Freud's Oedipus.

10. I want to repeat here my earlier acknowledgment (note 7) that Lacan does accept, with substantial revision, Freud's idea of the Oedipus complex. Total understanding of Lacan's revision would require additional discussion of Lacan's concepts of the Imaginary, the Real, and the Symbolic, which would take too much space and is unnecessary here. In essence, Lacan replaces Freud's biologism with cultural imperatives. Lacan associates the castration threat with the name of the Father who demands that the child separate from his/her experience of maternal plenitude and take his/her place in society. But as Madelon Sprengnether explains, Lacan's theory of child development still retains Freud's ordering of the Oedipal and preoedipal periods, although he presents this hierarchy as a function of language rather than of sexual difference (*The Spectral Mother: Freud, Feminism, and Psychoanalysis* [Ithaca: Cornell UP, 1990] 195). Thus, as Ellie Ragland-Sullivan points out, Lacan views the incest taboo not as a prohibition against the mother's body per se but as "an injunction to identify with the cultural order, which represents difference or otherness or individuation" ("Seeking the Third Term: Desire, the Phallus, and the Materiality of Language," *Feminism and Psychoanalysis*, ed. Richard Feldstein and Judith Roof [Ithaca: Cornell UP, 1989] 61).

11. In a sustained psychoanalytic interpretation of *Oedipus the King*, Morton Kaplan and Robert Kloss argue that Oedipus knew he had fulfilled the oracle but repressed that knowledge ("Fantasy of Innocence: Sophocles' *Oedipus the King*," *The Unspoken Motive: A Guide to Psychoanalytic Literary Criticism* [New York: Free, 1973] 105–18).

12. Sigmund Freud, qtd. in Lionel Trilling, "Freud and Literature," *The Liberal Imagination* (New York: Scribner's, 1950) 34.

13. Stuart Burns, "The Evolution of *Wise Blood*," *Modern Fiction Studies* 16 (1970): 147–62.

14. Burns 157.

15. Thomas LeClair, "Flannery O'Connor's *Wise Blood*: The Oedipal Theme," *Mississippi Quarterly* 29 (1976): 197–205.

16. LeClair 201.

17. Indeed, from a psychoanalytic perspective, one could argue that Haze's grandfather represents the father in whom the young son sees the threat of castration and is consequently forced to leave the mother's embrace and develop the monitoring superego. Hence, the grandfather's strong connection to Haze's conscience suggests that Haze has successfully worked through the Oedipal phase of his development.

18. Flannery O'Connor, letter to Eileen Hall, 10 March 1956, *Letters of Flannery O'Connor: The Habit of Being*, ed. Sally Fitzgerald (1979; New York: Vintage, 1980) 143.

19. Flannery O'Connor, "The Nature and Aim of Fiction," *Mystery and Manners*, ed. Sally Fitzgerald and Robert Fitzgerald (New York: Farrar, 1969) 72.

20. Ben Satterfield partly misses the point of this passage, I think, when he says that "no reader can state positively what, if anything, Haze sees other than what the text specifies, which is 'the blank gray sky that went on, depth after depth, into space'" ("*Wise Blood*, Artistic Anemia, and the Hemorrhaging of O'Connor Criticism," *Studies in American Fiction* 17.1 [1989]: 39). While I agree that the text does not provide an absolute meaning for this blank space and that readers go too far when they see redemption in this scene, Haze's actions after this moment *do* reveal that the space has had meaning for him. His complete reversal about Christianity—or rather, his return to what O'Connor wants us to believe is his true self—allows us to infer that Haze's experience at the embankment has led him to self-understanding, to an anagnorisis, like Oedipus', which forces him to recognize the truth about himself.

21. O'Connor, "The Nature and Aim of Fiction" 72.

22. Robert Fitzgerald, introduction, *Everything That Rises Must Converge*, by Flannery O'Connor (New York: Farrar, 1956) 13.

23. Ulrich Weisstein, *Max Frisch* (New York: Twayne, 1967) 70.

24. A phrase used by Frisch reporting on the novel in general in his unpublished notebooks; qtd. in Weisstein 74.

25. Michael Butler, *The Novels of Max Frisch* (London: Wolff, 1976) 106.

26. Lacan's notion of "the Other" is complicated and, as Anthony Wilden points out, impossible to define in any definite way,

since for Lacan, it has functional value, representing both the "significant other" to whom the neurotic's demands are addressed (the appeal of the Other), as well as the internalization of the Other (we desire what the

Other desires) and the unconscious subject itself or himself (the unconscious is the discourse of—or from—the Other). In another context, it will simply mean the category of "Otherness," a translation Lacan has himself employed. Sometimes "the Other" refers to the parents . . . , yet it is never a *person*. Very often the term seems to refer simply to the unconscious itself, although the unconscious is most often described as "the locus of the Other." (263–64)

While agreeing that the term is polysemous, Malcolm Bowie believes that in all its incarnations "the Other" is "that which introduces 'lack' and 'gap' into the operations of the subject and which, in doing so, incapacitates the subject for selfhood, or inwardness, or apperception, or plenitude; it guarantees the indestructibility of desire by keeping the goals in perpetual flight" ("Jacques Lacan," *Structuralism and Since: From Lévi-Strauss to Derrida*, ed. John Sturrock [Oxford: Oxford UP, 1979] 134).

27. Lacan, *Le Séminaire, livre II* 267; qtd. in Felman 129.

28. Felman 131.

29. Lacan, *Le Séminaire, livre II* 267; qtd. in Felman 131.

30. In fact, Butor's novel might fit equally well in this chapter, especially if one were to view Revel's burning of the map of Bleston as a symbolic patricide. However, I do not see such symbolism in that act of arson, and the pervasive allusions to the detective story in *Passing Time* further confirm its place in chapter 4.

31. As related by Stanley Edgar Hyman in his "On *The Interpretation of Dreams*," *Freud: A Collection of Critical Essays*, ed. Perry Meisel (Englewood Cliffs, NJ: Prentice, 1981) 124n; rpt. from Hyman's *The Tangled Bank: Darwin, Marx, Frazer and Freud as Imaginative Writers* (New York: Atheneum, 1962).

32. Of course, these works differ significantly from the analytic session in that they omit the presence of the analyst from the subject's writing and naming. Self-analysis is always dangerous and its conclusions doubtful, even when undertaken by such a perceptive subject as Freud. I am not, however, drawing an exact parallel between the plots of these novels and the psychoanalytic session. Rather, I am remarking on their salient similarities in the same way that Freud—and Lacan after him—remarked on the similarities between the action of *Oedipus the King* and the psychoanalytic session.

33. Butler 106.

34. Alan Latta, "Walter Faber and the Allegorization of Life: A Reading of Max Frisch's Novel *Homo Faber*," *Germanic Review* 54 (1979): 152–59.

35. Latta 154. Much of Faber's report is written after his meeting with Sabeth, but because he comes to appreciate the depth of his feelings for her only when he writes about her, his narrative acquires an accuracy of tone—

moving from the impersonal to the sentimental—that it would have lacked had this appreciation come before or with her death. In other words, Faber grows to self-realization during the writing of his narrative, and thus his report allows us to witness this growth from self-deception to self-awareness.

36. After he blinds himself, Oedipus says to the Chorus:

> Cursed be the benefactor
> That loosed my feet and gave me life
> For death; a poor exchange.
> Death would have been a boon
> To me and all of mine.
> *(Oedipus the King* 63)

37. According to Felman and in her words, 150.

38. Felman 146.

39. Although these three novels provide the most interesting and comprehensive look at the post-Freudian reworking of the Oedipus myth, they are not the only stories in this century that have used the myth in a psychological or psychoanalytic context. For example, Stratis Myrivilis' "The Cat's Eye" (1956) employs the self-blinding mytheme as a catalyst (no pun intended) when its central character, Nella, becomes obsessed with Sophocles' description of Oedipus' stabbing of his eyes. She finally exorcises this fixation by piercing the eye of her cat. Nella is diagnosed as having suffered a psychoneurotic crisis, which is now ended. Another twentieth-century novel that might fit in this chapter is John Barth's *Giles Goat-Boy* (1965), which contains one of the most humorous parodies of both Sophocles and Freud in "Taliped Decanus," the play within the novel. However, for his main plot, Barth is more interested in the hero myth as delineated by Lord Raglan and Joseph Campbell than in the Oedipus myth specifically. This preeminent interest in the hero myth is also shared by Ralph Ellison's *Invisible Man* (1952), although Ellison's revisions of certain mythemes from that myth can be profitably read as an attempt to mark Freud's interpretation of Oedipus' story with race and racism. Finally, a novel that seems to combine Freud's reading of Oedipus with Lacan's reading is Colin Spencer's *Asylum* (1966). This work explodes and parodies Freud's proposal by taking the latter half of it—the half Lacan stresses—literally, by actually putting the psychoanalytic session in the theatre. The principle behind Spencer's Institute for the Cure and Rehabilitation of Mental Diseases is that art can eliminate psychosis; the Institute's modus operandi is drama. The result is to reveal psychoanalysis as the true theatre of the absurd as the patients get stuck in reenacting the myths that supposedly inform their lives and as the doctors behave more insanely than their patients.

40. Green 236.
41. The term *family romance* has been variously—and ambiguously— used. Here I am using it to refer to any story in which Freud's interpretation of the mythemes of incest or patricide supply the main conflict, regardless of whether that conflict includes some desire on the part of the child to break from the parents or to fantasize about another family life. Such stories include Rebecca West's *The Judge* (1922); Henry Roth's *Call It Sleep* (1934); Frank O'Connor's "My Oedipus Complex" (1950); Louis Gallo's "Oedipus-Schmoedipus" (1961); and David Lang's *Oedipus Burning* (1981).
42. Indeed, Freud, too, embraced this symbolism. As Lowell Edmunds points out, Freud's followers made him aware that Oedipus' self-blinding could be symbolically equated with self-castration; however, Freud eventually backed away from such symbolism, preferring to have the self-blinding stand for a tragic insight that results from the analytic session. Edmunds concludes that there is a "fundamental division in both of Freud's two canonical statements of the Oedipus Complex between the Oedipus Complex as an aspect of childhood development and the Oedipus Complex as the cornerstone of psychoanalysis, as the inevitable discovery in every analysis" ("Freud and the Father: Oedipus Complex and Oedipus Myth," *Psychoanalysis and Contemporary Thought* 8 [1985]: 97). My thesis throughout this chapter has been that O'Connor, Frisch, and Moravia (as well as some recent psychoanalysts) have focused on the latter part of this division (discovery) rather than the former (development). What this amounts to, in effect, is a righting of the imbalance in the popular understanding of Freud.

6. The Epistemology of the Oedipus Myth

1. Righter 41–42.
2. Cameron vii. Although Cameron was writing over twenty years ago, his assertion about the popularity of *Oedipus the King* still seems to hold true. For example, the BBC produced all three of Sophocles' Theban plays in 1988; the Stratford Festival in Toronto, Canada, presented a double bill, *Oedipus/The Critic*, held July 30–September 4, 1988; and during the summer of 1988, the Williamstown Theatre Festival staged *The Legend of Oedipus*, a compilation of the Theban legend as told by Aeschylus, Sophocles, and Euripides, and written by Kenneth Cavander. The continued interest in Oedipus can also be found in theatrical productions such as Lee Breuer's *The Gospel of Colonus*, a Christian musical performed by African Americans and based on *Oedipus at Colonus*, which premiered in 1983.
3. Doty 30.

4. For another recent proposal—that of Vladimir Propp—see note 13, Introduction.

5. I am aware that my divisions are not completely pure, since, within my argument, syntactic, semantic, and pragmatic matters constantly overlap and bleed into one another. In reality, these fields are never mutually exclusive, and linguists have also commented on the artificiality of their boundaries. For instance, Roman Jakobson writes, "Attempts to construct a model of language without any relation either to the speaker or to the hearer and thus to hypostatize a code detached from actual communication threaten to make a scholastic fiction of language" ("Linguistics and Communication Theory," *The Structure of Language and Its Mathematical Aspects*, Proceedings of Symposia in Applied Mathematics 12 [New York: American Mathematical Soc., 1961] 245–52). Likewise, Carol Kane observes that "no grammar is 'descriptively adequate,' because a speaker must also take into account unsystematic, contextual factors that condition linguistic intuitions in an essential way. It is for this reason . . . that it is not possible to describe in advance all of the surface regularities of utterances or to define a set of possible sentences of a language" (*Pragmatics and Semantics: An Empiricist Theory* [Ithaca: Cornell UP, 1980] 34). The interdependence of the three fields is perhaps most clearly revealed by the fact that descriptive linguists are never unfamiliar with or incompetent in the language they analyze. Surely the identification of language structures (syntactics) and meaning (semantics) is predicated on the linguist's language experience (pragmatics).

6. One other precaution—or admission—seems in order. As I note throughout this study, most interpretations of the Oedipal mythemes are mine, especially in chapters 3–5. While I believe these interpretations to be valid and meaningful, I recognize that others may find them idiosyncratic or untenable. My focus here on the encoding side of the communication act—by examining mythemes found in twentieth-century fiction—makes these objections irrelevant. However, even such a focus cannot guarantee that I will solve this problem of subjectivity since recognizing signs—and changes in them—is also an activity of the decoder.

7. See note 25 in chapter 2.

8. Terence Turner, for example, delineates the numerous paradoxes and ironies that pervade, predicate, and propel the action of *Oedipus the King*, most of them having to do with inversions related to what Oedipus thinks he knows: "'Knowledge' is a central theme of the whole story of Oedipus (the riddle of the Sphinx, the oracle, and Oedipus's original quest to discover the identities of his parents are other manifestations of them)." Turner adds that the symbolic meaning of "knowledge" within the context of the story can be seen in the fact that "the male characters who acquire knowledge (Oedipus and Teiresias) either become blind or withdraw 'from the sight of

men', while the females (the Sphinx and Jocasta) who acquire it commit suicide" ("Oedipus: Time and Structure in Narrative Form," *Forms of Symbolic Action: Proceedings of the 1969 Annual Spring Meeting of the American Ethnological Society*, ed. Robert F. Spencer [Seattle: U of Washington P, 1969] 53).

9. Knox 137.

10. Knox 194.

11. Dodds 76–77.

12. Frank McConnell, *The Science Fiction of H. G. Wells* (New York: Oxford UP, 1981) 66.

13. McConnell 67.

14. Bertrand Russell, *Human Knowledge: Its Scope and Limits* (New York: Simon, 1948) 507.

15. Jacques Lacan, *Le Séminaire, livre XX: Encore* (Paris: Seuil, 1975) 88; qtd. in Felman, "Psychoanalysis and Education: Teaching Terminable and Interminable," chap. 4, *Jacques Lacan and the Adventure of Insight* 77.

16. Michael J. O'Brien, introduction, *Twentieth Century Interpretations of Oedipus Rex: A Collection of Critical Essays*, ed. O'Brien (Englewood Cliffs, NJ: Prentice, 1968) 11.

17. David Grossvogel, *Mystery and Its Fictions: From Oedipus to Agatha Christie* (Baltimore: Johns Hopkins UP, 1979) 178.

18. Oedipus' first four lines in *Oedipus at Colonus* are interrogative, and his questions pervade the entire drama.

19. René Girard, "Tiresias and the Critic," *The Structuralist Controversy: The Languages of Criticism and the Sciences of Man*, ed. Richard Macksey and Eugenio Donato (1970; Baltimore: Johns Hopkins UP, 1972) 19–20.

Works Cited

■

Ahl, Frederick. *Sophocles' Oedipus: Evidence and Self-Conviction.* Ithaca: Cornell UP, 1991.

Ancona, Francesco Aristide. *Writing the Absence of the Father: Undoing Oedipal Structures in the Contemporary American Novel.* Lanham, MD: UP of America, 1986.

Awad, L. *The Theme of Prometheus in English and French Literature: A Study of Literary Influence.* Cairo: n.p., 1963.

Baldanza, Frank. "The Classicism of Alberto Moravia." *Modern Fiction Studies* 3 (1957): 309–20.

———. "Mature Moravia." *Contemporary Literature* 9 (1968): 507–21.

Baldick, Chris, ed. *In Frankenstein's Shadow: Myth, Monstrosity, and Nineteenth-Century Writing.* Oxford: Oxford UP, 1986.

Barthes, Roland. "Myth Today." *Mythologies.* Trans. Annette Lavers. New York: Hill, 1972.

Bergonzi, Bernard. *The Early H. G. Wells: A Study of the Scientific Romances.* Manchester: Manchester UP, 1961.

Bernal, Olga. *Alain Robbe-Grillet: le roman de l'absence.* Paris: Gallimard, [1964].

Bleich, David. *Readers and Feelings: An Introduction to Subjective Criticism.* Urbana: NCTE, 1975.

———. *Subjective Criticism.* Baltimore: Johns Hopkins UP, 1978.

Blumenberg, Hans. *Work on Myth.* Trans. Robert M. Wallace. Cambridge: MIT P, 1985.

Bowie, Malcolm. "Jacques Lacan." *Structuralism and Since: From Lévi-Strauss to Derrida.* Ed. John Sturrock. Oxford: Oxford UP, 1979. 116–53.

Brizzi, Mary T. *Philip José Farmer.* Mercer Island, WA: Starmont, 1980.

Brock, Robert. "Robbe-Grillet's *Les Gommes* and Graham Greene's *This Gun for Hire*: Imitation or Initiation." *Modern Fiction Studies* 29 (1983): 688–94.

Works Cited

Brombert, Victor. "A Victim Was Waiting." *New York Times Book Review* 18 Oct. 1964: 4.

Brooks, Peter. *Reading for the Plot*. 1984. New York: Vintage, 1985.

Brower, Reuben A. "Visual and Verbal Translation of Myth: Neptune in Virgil, Rubens, Dryden." *Myth, Symbol, and Culture*. Ed. Clifford Geertz. New York: Norton: 1971. 155–82.

Burns, Stuart. "The Evolution of *Wise Blood*." *Modern Fiction Studies* 16 (1970): 147–62.

Butler, Michael. *The Novels of Max Frisch*. London: Wolff, 1976.

Butor, Michel. *Passing Time*. Trans. Jean Stewart. London: Faber, 1961. London: Calder, 1965.

Buxton, R. G. A. "Blindness and Limits: Sophocles and the Logic of Myth." *Journal of Hellenic Studies* 100 (1980): 22–37.

Caesar, Terry P. "A Note on Pynchon's Naming." *Pynchon Notes* 5 (1981): 5–10.

Cameron, Alister. *The Identity of Oedipus the King*. New York: New York UP, 1968.

Cassirer, Ernst. *Language and Myth*. Trans. Suzanne Langer. New York: Harper, 1946.

Chadwick, A. R., and Virginia Harger-Grinling. "Mythic Structures in Alain Robbe-Grillet's *Les Gommes*." *International Fiction Review* 2 (1984): 102–4.

Chase, Richard. *Quest for Myth*. Baton Rouge: Louisiana State UP, 1949.

Chodorow, Nancy. *The Reproduction of Mothering: Psychoanalysis and the Sociology of Gender*. Berkeley: U of California P, 1978.

Cocking, J. M. "The 'Noveau Roman' in France." *Essays in French Literature* 2 (1965): 1–14.

Cook, Albert. *Myth and Language*. Bloomington: Indiana UP, 1980.

Cooper, Peter. *Signs and Symptoms: Thomas Pynchon and the Contemporary World*. Berkeley: U of California P, 1983.

Coward, Rosalind, and John Ellis. *Language and Materialism: Developments in Semiology and the Theory of Signs*. London: Routledge, 1977.

Culler, Jonathan. *Structuralist Poetics: Structuralism, Linguistics, and the Study of Literature*. Ithaca: Cornell UP, 1975.

Dabezies, André. *Visages de Faust au XXe siècle: littérature, idéologie, et mythe*. Paris: Presses Universitaires de France, 1967.

Davies, Rosemary. "The Mother as Destroyer: Psychic Division in the Writings of D. H. Lawrence." *The D. H. Lawrence Review* 13 (1980): 220–38.

De Lauretis, Teresa. *Alice Doesn't: Feminism, Semiotics, Cinema*. Bloomington: Indiana UP, 1984.

Delcourt, Marie. *Oedipe ou la légende du conquérant*. Paris: Société d'Édition des Belles Lettres, 1944.

152

Deleuze, Gilles, and Félix Guattari. *Anti-Oedipus: Capitalism and Schizophrenia.* Trans. Robert Hurley, Mark Seem, and Helen R. Lane. New York: Viking, 1977.

Detienne, Marcel. *The Creation of Mythology.* Trans. Margaret Cook. Chicago: U of Chicago P, 1986.

De Voto, Bernard. "Freud's Influence on Literature." *Saturday Review of Literature* 20 (1939): 10–11.

De Weever, Jacqueline. *Mythmaking and Metaphor in Black Women's Fiction.* New York: St. Martin's, 1991.

Dick, Philip, and Roger Zelazny. *Deus Irae.* New York: Dell, 1976.

Dodds, E. R. "On Misunderstanding the *Oedipus Rex.*" *The Ancient Concept of Progress and Other Essays on Greek Literature and Belief.* Oxford: Oxford UP, 1973. 64–77.

Doty, William G. *Mythography: The Study of Myths and Rituals.* Tuscaloosa: U of Alabama P, 1986.

Dundes, Alan, ed. *The Flood Myth.* Berkeley: U of California P, 1988.

———. "Structuralism and Folklore." *Studia Fennica* 20 (1976): 75–93. Rpt. in *Essays in Folkloristics.* Meerut: Folklore Institute, 1978. 178–206.

Eco, Umberto. *The Role of the Reader: Explorations in the Semiotics of Texts.* Bloomington: Indiana UP, 1979.

———. *Semiotics and the Philosophy of Language.* Bloomington: Indiana UP, 1984.

Edmunds, Lowell. "Freud and the Father: Oedipus Complex and Oedipus Myth." *Psychoanalysis and Contemporary Thought* 8 (1985): 87–102.

Ehrenberg, V. *Sophocles and Pericles.* Oxford: Oxford UP, 1954.

Eliot, George. *The Mill on the Floss.* Ed. Gordon S. Haight. Boston: Houghton, 1961.

Eliot, T. S. "Ulysses, Order, and Myth." *The Dial* 75 (1923): 480–83. Rpt. as "Myth and Literary Classicism." *The Modern Tradition.* Ed. Richard Ellmann and Charles Feidelson, Jr. New York: Oxford UP, 1965. 679–81.

Euripides. *The Phoenician Women. Euripides V.* Trans. Elizabeth Wycoff. Chicago: Phoenix-U of Chicago P, 1959. 72–140.

Fabrizio, Richard. "The Complex Oedipus: The Oedipus Figure in European Literature." Diss. New York U, 1967.

Farmer, Philip José. "Riders of the Purple Wage: Or the Great Gavage." *Dangerous Visions: 33 Original Stories.* Ed. Harlan Ellison. Garden City, NY: Doubleday, 1967. 33–104.

——— [Kilgore Trout, pseud.]. *Venus on the Half-Shell.* New York: Dell, 1974.

Faulkner, William. "Session Nine." *Faulkner in the University: Class Conferences at the University of Virginia 1957–1958.* Ed. Frederick L.

Gwynn and Joseph L. Blotner. 1959. New York: Vintage, 1965. 71–81.

Fawcett, Edgar. "Oedipus and the Sphinx." *North American Review* 175 (1902): 871–76.

Feder, Lillian. *Ancient Myth in Modern Poetry*. Princeton: Princeton UP, 1971.

Felman, Shoshana. *Jacques Lacan and the Adventure of Insight: Psychoanalysis in Contemporary Culture*. Cambridge: Harvard UP, 1987.

Fish, Stanley. Headnote. "What Is Stylistics and Why Are They Saying Such Terrible Things about It?" *Is There a Text in This Class? The Authority of Interpretive Communities*. Cambridge: Harvard UP, 1980. 68–96.

Fitzgerald, Robert. Introduction. *Everything That Rises Must Converge*. By Flannery O'Connor. New York: Farrar, 1956. vii–xxxiv.

Fitzgerald, Sally, ed. *Letters of Flannery O'Connor: The Habit of Being*. 1979. New York: Vintage: 1980.

Foucault, Michel. *The Discourse on Language*. Trans. Rupert Swyer. *The Archaeology of Knowledge and The Discourse on Language*. New York: Pantheon, 1972. 215–37.

Fredericks, Casey. *The Future of Eternity: Mythologies of Science Fiction and Fantasy*. Bloomington: Indiana UP, 1982.

———. "Revivals of Ancient Mythologies in Current Science Fiction and Fantasy." *Many Futures, Many Worlds: Theme and Form in Science Fiction*. Ed. Thomas D. Clareson. Kent, OH: Kent State UP, 1977. 50–65.

Freud, Sigmund. *The Interpretation of Dreams*. Trans. and ed. James Strachey. New York: Avon, 1965.

———. "On the Universal Tendency to Debasement in the Sphere of Love (Contributions to the Psychology of Love, II) (1912)." *The Standard Edition of the Complete Psychological Works of Sigmund Freud*. Trans. and ed. James Strachey. Vol. 11. London: Hogarth, 1957. 177–90. 24 vols. 1953–74.

———. "A Special Type of Choice of Object Made by Men (Contributions to the Psychology of Love, I) (1910)." *The Standard Edition of the Complete Psychological Works of Sigmund Freud*. Trans. and ed. James Strachey. Vol. 11. London: Hogarth, 1957. 163–75. 24 vols. 1953–74.

Freud, Sigmund, and Josef Breuer. *Studies on Hysteria*. Vol. 2 of *The Standard Edition of the Complete Psychological Works of Sigmund Freud*. Trans. and ed. James Strachey. London: Hogarth, 1955. 24 vols. 1953–74.

Frisch, Max. *Homo Faber*. Trans. Michael Bullock. New York: Harcourt, 1959.

Works Cited

Frye, Northrop. "Literature and Myth." *Relations of Literary Study*. Ed. James Thorpe. New York: MLA, 1967. 27–41.

Galinsky, G. K. *The Heracles Theme*. Oxford: Oxford UP, 1972.

Girard, René. "Tiresias and the Critic." *The Structuralist Controversy: The Languages of Criticism and the Sciences of Man*. Ed. Richard Macksey and Eugenio Donato. 1970. Baltimore: Johns Hopkins UP, 1972. 15–21.

Gould, Eric. *Mythical Intentions in Modern Literature*. Princeton: Princeton UP, 1981.

Green, André. *The Tragic Effect: The Oedipus Complex in Tragedy*. Trans. Alan Sheridan. Cambridge: Cambridge UP, 1979.

Grella, George. "Murder and Manners: The Formal Detective Novel." *Novel* 4 (1970): 30–48.

Grossvogel, David. *Mystery and Its Fictions: From Oedipus to Agatha Christie*. Baltimore: Johns Hopkins UP, 1979.

Hamilton, Victoria. *Narcissus and Oedipus: The Children of Psychoanalysis*. London: Routledge, 1982.

Harrison, Jane. *Prolegomena to the Study of Greek Religion*. 2nd ed. Cambridge: Cambridge UP, 1908.

Hawkes, Terence. *Structuralism and Semiotics*. London: Methuen, 1977.

Haycraft, Howard, ed. *The Art of the Mystery Story*. New York: Simon, 1946.

Haynes, Roslynn. *H. G. Wells: Discoverer of the Future: The Influence of Science on His Thought*. London: Macmillan, 1980.

Hennelly, Mark, Jr. "*The Time Machine*: A Romance of 'The Human Heart.'" *Extrapolation* 20 (1979): 154–67.

Herman, Judith, and Lisa Hirschman. "Father-Daughter Incest." *Signs: Journal of Women in Culture and Society* 2.4 (1977): 735–56.

Hirsch, E. D. *The Aims of Interpretation*. Chicago: U of Chicago P, 1976.

Hjortsberg, William. *Falling Angel*. New York: Harcourt, 1978.

Hoffman, Frederick J. *Freudianism and the Literary Mind*. 2nd ed. Baton Rouge: Louisiana State UP, 1957.

Holquist, Michael. "Whodunit and Other Questions: Metaphysical Detective Stories in Post-War Fiction." *New Literary History* 3 (1971): 135–56.

Horton, Andrew Steele, Jr. "The Oedipus Tyrannus Theme in Western Literature." Diss. U of Illinois at Champaign-Urbana, 1973.

Huntington, John. *The Logic of Fantasy: H. G. Wells and Science Fiction*. New York: Columbia UP, 1982.

Huss, Roy. "Appendix B: The 'Complexes' of Art: Some Contributions Made by Myth and Literature to the Language of Psychoanalysis." *The Mindscapes of Art: Dimensions of the Psyche in Fiction, Drama, and Film*. Rutherford: Fairleigh Dickinson UP, 1986.

Works Cited

Hyman, Stanley Edgar. "On *The Interpretation of Dreams.*" *The Tangled Bank: Darwin, Marx, Frazer and Freud as Imaginative Writers.* New York: Atheneum, 1962. 310–38. Rpt. in *Freud: A Collection of Critical Essays.* Ed. Perry Meisel. Englewood Cliffs, NJ: Prentice, 1981. 121–44.

Iser, Wolfgang. *The Act of Reading: A Theory of Aesthetic Response.* Trans. David Henry Wilson. Baltimore: Johns Hopkins UP, 1978.

———. "Der Archetyp als Leerform. Erzählschablonen und Kommunikation in Joyces *Ulysses.*" *Terror und Spiel. Probleme der Mythenrezeption.* Ed. Manfred Fuhrmann. *Poetik und Hermeneutik* 4. Munich: Fink Verlag, 1971. 369–408. Trans. and rpt. as "Patterns of Communication in Joyce's *Ulysses.*" *The Implied Reader: Patterns of Communication in Prose Fiction from Bunyan to Beckett.* By Iser. Baltimore: Johns Hopkins UP, 1974. 196–233.

Jakobson, Roman. "Linguistics and Communication Theory." *The Structure of Language and Its Mathematical Aspects.* Proceedings of Symposia in Applied Mathematics 12. New York: American Mathematical Soc., 1961. 245–52.

Janeway, Elizabeth. "Incest: A Rational Look at the Oldest Taboo." *Ms.* 10 (1981): 61+.

Jefferson, Ann. *The Nouveau Roman and the Poetics of Fiction.* Cambridge: Cambridge UP, 1980.

Kane, Carol. *Pragmatics and Semantics: An Empiricist Theory.* Ithaca: Cornell UP, 1980.

Kaplan, Morton, and Robert Kloss. "Fantasy of Innocence: Sophocles' *Oedipus the King.*" *The Unspoken Motive: A Guide to Psychoanalytic Literary Criticism.* New York: Free, 1973. 105–18.

Ketterer, David. "Oedipus as Time Traveller." *Science-Fiction Studies* 9 (1982): 340–41.

Kirk, G. S. *The Nature of Greek Myths.* 1974. New York: Penguin, 1976.

Knox, Bernard. *Oedipus at Thebes.* New Haven: Yale UP, 1957.

Knox, Ronald A. "A Detective Story Decalogue." Haycraft 194–96.

Kushner, Eva. *Le mythe d'Orphée dans la littérature française contemporaine.* Paris: Nizet, 1961.

Lacan, Jacques. *Le Séminaire, livre II: Le moi dans la théorie de Freud et dans la technique psychoanalytique.* Paris: Seuil, 1978.

———. *Le Séminaire, livre XX: Encore.* Paris: Seuil, 1975.

———. *Speech and Language in Psychoanalysis.* Trans. and ed. Anthony Wilden. 1968. Baltimore: Johns Hopkins UP, 1981.

Lake, David. "The White Sphinx and the Whitened Lemur: Images of Death in *The Time Machine.*" *Science-Fiction Studies* 6 (1979): 77–84.

Works Cited

Lapointe, François H., and Clair C. Lapointe, eds. *Claude Lévi-Strauss and His Critics: An International Bibliography of Criticism (1950–1976)*. New York: Garland, 1977.

Latta, Alan. "Walter Faber and the Allegorization of Life: A Reading of Max Frisch's Novel *Homo Faber*." *Germanic Review* 54 (1979): 152–59.

Lazarsfeld, Sophie. "Did Oedipus Have an Oedipus Complex?" *American Journal of Orthopsychiatry* 14 (1944): 226–29.

LeClair, Thomas. "Flannery O'Connor's *Wise Blood*: The Oedipal Theme." *Mississippi Quarterly* 29 (1976): 197–205.

Lévi-Strauss, Claude. "A Structural Study of Myth." *Structural Anthropology*. Trans. Claire Jacobson and Brooke Grundfest Schoepf. New York: Basic, 1963. 206–31.

Longley, John Lewis, Jr. "Joe Christmas: The Hero in the Modern World." *The Tragic Mask: A Study of Faulkner's Heroes*. Chapel Hill: U of North Carolina P, 1957. 192–205.

MacCannell, Juliet Flower. *Figuring Lacan: Criticism and the Cultural Unconscious*. London: Croom Helm, 1986.

McConnell, Frank. *The Science Fiction of H. G. Wells*. New York: Oxford UP, 1981.

Mendelson, Edward. "The Sacred, the Profane, and *The Crying of Lot 49*." *Pynchon: A Collection of Critical Essays*. Ed. Mendelson. Englewood Cliffs, NJ: Prentice, 1978. 112–46.

Mercier, Vivian. *The New Novel: From Queneau to Pinget*. New York: Farrar, 1971.

Merivale, Patricia. *Pan the Goat-God: His Myth in Modern Times*. Cambridge: Harvard UP, 1969.

Messer, Alfred. "The 'Phaedra Complex.'" *Archives of General Psychiatry* 21 (1969): 213–18.

Mitchell, Giles. "*Sons and Lovers* and the Oedipal Project." *The D. H. Lawrence Review* 13 (1980): 209–19.

Moddelmog, Debra A. "Faulkner's Theban Saga: *Light in August*." *The Southern Literary Journal* 18.1 (1985): 13–29.

Moravia, Alberto. *The Lie*. Trans. Angus Davidson. New York: Farrar, 1966.

Morrissette, Bruce. "Oedipus and Existentialism: *Les Gommes* of Robbe-Grillet." *Wisconsin Studies in Contemporary Literature* 1 (1960): 43–73. Rev. and rpt. as "Oedipus or the Closed Circle: *The Erasers* (1953)." *The Novels of Robbe-Grillet*. Trans. Morrissette. Ithaca: Cornell UP, 1975. 38–74.

Mullahy, Patrick. *Oedipus Myth and Complex: A Review of Psychoanalytic Theory*. 1948. New York: Grove, 1955.

Neumann, Erich. *The Origins and History of Consciousness*. Trans. R. F. C. Hull. Bollingen Series 42. Princeton: Princeton UP, 1970.

Works Cited

Nordquist, Joan, comp. *Claude Lévi-Strauss: A Bibliography*. Santa Cruz, CA: Reference and Research Services, 1987.

O'Brien, Michael J. Introduction. *Twentieth Century Interpretations of Oedipus Rex: A Collection of Critical Essays*. Ed. O'Brien. Englewood Cliffs, NJ: Prentice, 1968. 1–16.

O'Connor, Flannery. "The Nature and Aim of Fiction." *Mystery and Manners*. Ed. Sally Fitzgerald and Robert Fitzgerald. New York: Farrar, 1969. 63–86.

———. *Wise Blood*. *Three By Flannery O'Connor: Wise Blood, A Good Man Is Hard to Find, The Violent Bear It Away*. New York: NAL, n.d. 9–126.

Olivier, Christiane. *Jocasta's Children: The Imprint of the Mother*. Trans. George Craig. London: Routledge, 1989.

O'Neill, Kathleen. "On *Passing Time*." *Mosaic* 8 (1974): 29–37.

Orr, Leonard. "From Procrustean Criticism to Process Hermeneutics." *Substance* 25 (1980): 74–86.

Parry, John. *The Psychology of Human Communication*. New York: American Elsevier, 1968.

Patai, Raphael. "Myth Interpretation Through the Ages." *Myth and Modern Man*. Englewood Cliffs, NJ: Prentice, 1972. 10–46.

Perry, Menakhem. "Literary Dynamics: How the Order of a Text Creates Its Meanings, with an Analysis of Faulkner's 'A Rose for Emily.'" *Poetics Today* 1.1–2 (1979): 35–64, 311–61.

Phelan, James. *Reading People, Reading Plots: Character, Progression, and the Interpretation of Narrative*. Chicago: U of Chicago P, 1989.

Phillips, D. Z. "What the Complex Did to Oedipus." *Through a Darkening Glass: Philosophy, Literature, and Cultural Change*. Notre Dame: U of Notre Dame P, 1982. 82–88.

Politzer, Heinz. "Hatte Ödipus einen Ödipus-Komplex?" *Psychologie in der Litteraturwissenschaft*. Ed. W. Paulsen. Heidelberg: Stiehm, 1971. 115–39.

Priestman, Martin. *Detective Fiction and Literature: The Figure on the Carpet*. London: Macmillan, 1990.

Propp, Vladimir. "Oedipus in the Light of Folklore." Trans. Polly Coote. *Oedipus: A Folklore Casebook*. Ed. Lowell Edmunds and Alan Dundes. New York: Garland, 1983. 76–121.

Pynchon, Thomas. *The Crying of Lot 49*. New York: Bantam, 1966.

Rabinowitz, Peter. *Before Reading: Narrative Conventions and the Politics of Interpretation*. Ithaca: Cornell UP, 1987.

Ragland-Sullivan, Ellie. *Jacques Lacan and the Philosophy of Psychoanalysis*. Urbana: U of Illinois P, 1986.

———. "Seeking the Third Term: Desire, the Phallus, and the Materiality of Language." *Feminism and Psychoanalysis*. Ed. Richard Feldstein and Judith Roof. Ithaca: Cornell UP, 1989. 40–64.

Rainwater, Catherine. "Encounters with the 'White Sphinx': Poe's Influence on Some Early Works of H. G. Wells." *English Literature in Transition* 26.1 (1983): 35–51.

Rank, Otto. *The Myth of the Birth of the Hero: A Psychological Interpretation of Mythology*. Trans. F. Robbins and Smith Ely Jelliffe. 1909. New York: Journal of Nervous and Mental Disease Pub. Co., 1914.

Righter, William. *Myth and Literature*. London: Routledge, 1975.

Robbe-Grillet, Alain. *The Erasers*. Trans. Richard Howard. New York: Grove, 1964.

Roudaut, Jean. *Michel Butor ou le livre futur*. Paris: Gallimard, 1964.

Rudnytsky, Peter. *Freud and Oedipus*. New York: Columbia UP, 1987.

Russell, Bertrand. *Human Knowledge: Its Scope and Limits*. New York: Simon, 1948.

Said, Edward. *Beginnings: Intention and Method*. New York: Basic, 1975.

Santraud, J. M. "Dans le sillage de la baleinière d'Arthur Gordon Pym: *Le sphinx des glaces, Dan Yack*." *Etudes Anglaises* 25 (1972): 353–66.

Satterfield, Ben. "*Wise Blood*, Artistic Anemia, and the Hemorrhaging of O'Connor Criticism." *Studies in American Fiction* 17.1 (1989): 33–50.

Saussure, Ferdinand de. *Course in General Linguistics*. Ed. Charles Bally and Albert Sechehaye. Trans. Wade Baskin. New York: Philosophical Library, 1959.

Scafella, Frank. "The White Sphinx and *The Time Machine*." *Science-Fiction Studies* 8 (1981): 255–65.

Schiller, F. S. C. *Riddles of the Sphinx: A Study in the Philosophy of Evolution*. 2nd ed. London: Swan Sonnenschein, 1894.

Scholes, Robert. *Semiotics and Interpretation*. New Haven: Yale UP, 1982.

———. *Structuralism in Literature*. New Haven: Yale UP, 1974.

Sicard, M. I. *Don Juan: mythe et réalité*. Toulouse: Plon, 1967.

Slochower, Harry. *Mythopoesis: Mythic Patterns in the Literary Classics*. Detroit: Wayne State UP, 1970.

Smeed, J. M. *Faust in Literature*. London: Oxford UP, 1975.

Smith, Barbara Herrnstein. *Poetic Closure: A Study of How Poems End*. Chicago: U of Chicago P, 1968.

Sophocles. *The Theban Plays*. Trans. E. F. Watling. New York: Penguin, 1947.

Spanos, William V. "The Detective and the Boundary: Some Notes on the Post-modern Literary Imagination." *Boundary* 1 (1972): 147–68.

Sprengnether, Madelon. *The Spectral Mother: Freud, Feminism, and Psychoanalysis*. Ithaca: Cornell UP, 1990.

Works Cited

Stanford, W. B. *The Ulysses Theme: A Study in the Adaptability of a Traditional Hero.* 2nd ed. Ann Arbor: U of Michigan P, 1968.

Steig, Michael. *Stories of Reading: Subjectivity and Literary Understanding.* Baltimore: Johns Hopkins UP, 1989.

Steiner, George. *Antigones: How the Antigone Legend Has Endured in Western Literature, Art, and Thought.* Oxford: Clarendon, 1986.

Stoltzfus, Ben. *Alain Robbe-Grillet and the New French Novel.* Carbondale: Southern Illinois UP, 1964.

Strauss, Walter A. *Descent and Return: The Orphic Theme in Modern Literature.* Cambridge: Harvard UP, 1971.

Sturrock, John. *The French New Novel: Claude Simon, Michel Butor, Alain Robbe-Grillet.* London: Oxford UP, 1969.

Szanto, George. *Narrative Consciousness: Structure and Perception in the Fiction of Kafka, Beckett, and Robbe-Grillet.* Austin: U of Texas P, 1972.

Tani, Stefano. *The Doomed Detective: The Contribution of the Detective Novel to Postmodern American and Italian Fiction.* Carbondale: Southern Illinois UP, 1984.

Tanner, Tony. *Thomas Pynchon.* London: Methuen, 1982.

Thompson, Raymond. *The Return from Avalon: A Study of the Arthurian Legend in Modern Fiction.* Westport: Greenwood, 1985.

Todorov, Tzvetan. "The Typology of Detective Fiction." *The Poetics of Prose.* Trans. Richard Howard. Ithaca: Cornell UP, 1977. 42–52.

Trilling, Lionel. "Freud and Literature." *The Liberal Imagination.* New York: Scribner's, 1950. 34–57.

Trousson, Raymond. *Le thème de Prométhée dans la littérature européene.* 2 vols. Geneva: Librairie Droz, 1964.

Turner, Terence. "Narrative Structure and Mythopoesis: A Critique and Reformulation of Structuralist Concepts of Myth, Narrative and Poetics." *Arethusa* 10 (1977): 103–63.

———. "Oedipus: Time and Structure in Narrative Form." *Forms of Symbolic Action: Proceedings of the 1969 Annual Spring Meeting of the American Ethnological Society.* Ed. Robert F. Spencer. Seattle: U of Washington P, 1969. 26–68.

Twitchell, James B. *Forbidden Partners: The Incest Taboo in Modern Culture.* New York: Columbia UP, 1987.

Van Dine, S. S. "Twenty Rules for Writing Detective Stories." Haycraft 189–93.

Van Meter, Jan R. "Sophocles and the Rest of the Boys in the Pulps: Myth and the Detective Novel." *Dimensions of Detective Fiction.* Ed. Larry N. Landrum, Pat Browne, and Ray B. Browne. N.p.: Popular, 1976. 12–21.

Works Cited

Vellacott, Philip. *Sophocles and Oedipus: A Study of* Oedipus Tyrannus *with a New Translation*. Ann Arbor: U of Michigan P, 1971.

Verne, Jules. *An Antarctic Mystery*. Trans. Mrs. Cashel Hoey. Philadelphia: Lippincott, 1899. Boston: Hall, 1975.

Vickery, John. *Myths and Texts: Strategies of Incorporation and Displacement*. Baton Rouge: Louisiana State UP, 1983.

——. "Orpheus and Persephone: Uses and Meanings." *Classical Mythology in Twentieth-Century Thought and Literature*. Ed. Wendell M. Aycock and Theodore M. Klein. Lubbock: Texas Tech P, 1980. 187–212.

Watson, Robert N. "Who Bids for Tristero? The Conversion of Pynchon's Oedipa Maas." *Southern Humanities Review* 17 (1983): 59–75.

Watts, Cedric. "King Oedipus and the Toy-vendor." *Reconstructing Literature*. Ed. Laurence Lerner. Totowa, NJ: Barnes, 1983. 106–22.

Weinstein, Leo. *The Metamorphosis of Don Juan*. Stanford: Stanford UP, 1959.

Weisstein, Ulrich. *Max Frisch*. New York: Twayne, 1967.

Wells, H. G. *The Definitive* Time Machine: *A Critical Edition of H. G. Wells's Scientific Romance*. Ed. Harry M. Geduld. Bloomington: Indiana UP, 1987.

——. "Human Evolution, an Artificial Process." *Early Writings in Science and Science Fiction by H. G. Wells*. Ed. Robert M. Philmus and David Y. Hughes. Berkeley: U of California P, 1975. 211–19.

White, John. "Mythological Fiction and the Reading Process." *Literary Criticism and Myth*. Ed. Joseph P. Strelka. University Park: Penn State UP, 1980. 72–92.

——. *Mythology in the Modern Novel: A Study of Prefigurative Techniques*. Princeton: Princeton UP, 1971.

Wilden, Anthony. "Lacan and the Discourse of the Other." *Speech and Language in Psychoanalysis*. By Jacques Lacan. Trans. Anthony Wilden. Baltimore: Johns Hopkins UP, 1981. 159–311.

Young, James Dean. "The Enigma Variations of Thomas Pynchon." *Critique: Studies in Modern Fiction* 10.1 (1967): 69–77.

Ziolkowski, Theodore. *Fictional Transfigurations of Jesus*. Princeton: Princeton UP, 1972.

Index

■

163

Index

Index

Kane, Carol, 148n.5
Kaplan, Morton, and Robert Kloss, 87–88, 143n.11
Kirk, G. S., 1, 2
Kloss, Robert. See Kaplan, Morton
Knowledge, 32, 83, 84, 99, 110–14, 136n.25, 143n.11, 148n.8. See also Epistemology; Self-knowledge
Knox, Bernard, 42, 111, 112, 133n.44
Knox, Ronald A., 138n.6
Kristeva, Julia, 9
Kuhn, Thomas, 112

Labdacus, 11
Lacan, Jacques, 93, 95, 96, 99, 113, 141n.1, 142n.7, 143n.10; concept of "the Other," 95, 144–45n.26; interpretation of Oedipus myth, 32, 33, 87–89, 95–96, 103, 132n.36, 143n.9, 145n.32, 146n.39
Laius, 10, 11, 12, 13, 42, 70, 74, 79, 88, 95
Lake, David, 47, 49
Lameness, 92
Lang, David: Oedipus Burning, 18, 147n.41
Latta, Alan, 96, 97
Lawrence, D. H., 18; Sons and Lovers, 35–36, 142n.3
Lear complex, 131n.24
LeClair, Thomas, 91
Legend, 122n.10
Levin, Ira: Rosemary's Baby, 141n.22
Lévi-Strauss, Claude, 6, 33; "A Structural Study of Myth," 10–11, 124n.16, 125n.27
Longley, John, 37–38

McConnell, Frank, 112
Mann, Thomas, xi, 18, 128n.11; Joseph and His Brothers, 8
Méconnaissance, 32, 88, 93, 94, 102
Medea complex, 29
Mendelson, Edward, 78
Merope, 12
Metaphysical detective fiction. See Antidetective fiction
Mitchell, Giles, 36
Moddelmog, Debra, 133n.47
Moravia, Alberto, xi, xiv, 24, 39, 106; The Conformist, 39; Conjugal Love, 39; Ghost at Noon, 39; The

Lie, 25–34, 39, 72, 88, 96, 101–3, 103–4, 108, 110, 147n.42
Morelli, Giovanni, 96
Morrissette, Bruce, 65–69, 140n.12
Moses, 82
Mother-son love, 7, 35. See also Incest
Mullahy, Patrick, xv
Myrivilis, Stratis, "The Cat's Eye," 146n.39
Myth: as language, 3, 5–12, 15, 107–8, 128n.11; definition, 1–4; difference from other tales, 122n.10; intertextuality of, 4–5, 11, 54
Mytheme, xiv, 9–14, 16, 17, 19, 20, 22–23, 25–29, 33–41, 54, 61, 107, 108, 123n.10, 125n.27, 126n.32, 127n.4, 128n.11; as indicator of authorial patterns, 39–40, 108; as indicator of societal concerns, 40, 105–15; changes in, 28–30, 33, 36, 37, 38, 108–9; definition, 9–14; explicit, 16, 19–34, 39, 67, 129n.13; implicit, 16, 20, 22, 24, 26, 27, 28, 34–40, 61, 67, 129n.13; Oedipal, xiv, 12–13, 19, 20, 22, 25–40, 41, 42, 52, 54, 59, 64, 67, 70, 77, 78, 87, 89, 94, 96, 102, 103, 104, 107–14, 126n.32, 129n.13, 133n.47, 133–34n.3, 140n.22, 142n.3, 146n.39, 148n.6; semantic encyclopedia of, 17, 36, 41, 87, 142n.3; weighted, 34–37
Mythic allusion. See Mythic signal
Mythicity, 2, 106, 122n.10
Mythic signal, 17–19, 34, 66, 67, 70, 128–29n.13

Narcissus, 7, 86
Neumann, Erich, 46

O'Brien, Michael, 113
O'Connor, Flannery, xi, xiv, 103, 105, 147n.42; Wise Blood, 36–37, 88, 90–95, 101, 103–4, 110, 113, 144n.20, 147n.42
O'Connor, Frank: "My Oedipus Complex," 18, 147n.41
Odysseus (Ulysses), 58, 120n.14; myth, 8
Oedipus complex, xiv, 30, 35, 39, 87, 89, 103, 104, 142n.2, 142–43n.7,

166

DEBRA A. MODDELMOG is an associate professor of English at The Ohio State University, where she teaches twentieth-century literature with a focus on multicultural and feminist issues. She has published articles on Ernest Hemingway, William Faulkner, Katherine Anne Porter, and Thomas Pynchon.